MAGIC MIRROR MARKETING:

YOUR PRACTICAL GUIDE TO BUSINESS MARKETING

www.MagicMirrorInvesting.com

LARRY YAKIWCZUK
PATRICK NG

Buckaru Publishing

www.BuckaruPublishing.com

6 BONUSES

5 Homes to Financial Freedom   FREE
A webinar recording explaining how you can achieve financial freedom with the equivalent cash flow of 80 rentals from owning just 5 homes. (Value of $49.99)
Visit **www.MagicMirrorInvesting.com/book**

Making Real Money With Joint Ventures   FREE
A webinar recording discussing the specifics about joint ventures and how they can be a short cut to vast residual profits with very little initial work. (Value of $49.99)
Visit **www.MagicMirrorInvesting.com/book**

Rent To Own with No Money and No Risk   FREE
A webinar recording with over 60 minutes on rent to own secrets and different ways to increase your profits and minimize risks in real estate investing. (Value of $49.99)
Visit **www.MagicMirrorInvesting.com/book**

A Millionaire's Mindset   FREE
A webinar recording giving you an insight into the mindset of a millionaire where you will learn a bit about business, real estate, and the stock market. (Value of $49.99)
Visit **www.MagicMirrorInvesting.com/book**

Power Investing   FREE

A webinar recording giving you an insight into the mindset of a Millionaire where you will learn a bit about the stock market and investing. (Value of $9.99)
Visit **www.MagicMirrorInvesting.com/book**

Educational Grants and Credits: FREE

We have a special educational grant program which helps students with the purchase of Advanced Educational materials. Also, any purchase of our related advanced educational programs or products, will result in the same amount returned as a fee credit on a major internet auction site that you can use for various listing upgrades or on site advertising. (Value up to $3,499.99)
Visit **www.MagicMirrorInvesting.com/book**

CONTENTS

Introduction   1

1 – Understand The "Demand" Of Market   5

2 – The "3 Steps Mastery" Marketing System   11

3 – The "Triple Power" Marketing Plan   29

4 – The "3 Growth Pillars" In Business   35

5 – How To Avoid The 3 Biggest Marketing Mistakes   43

6 – Connect With Your Audience Using
      E-zines, Flyers, And Receipts   63

7 – Grow Your Business By Organizing Events   77

8 – Cross-Marketing With Joint Venture   83

9 – Networking Is The Key To Your Marketing Success   89

10 – How To Use Newsletters For Your Marketing   95

About The Authors

    Patrick Ng   109

    Larry Yakiwzuk   111

Six Bonuses   117

INTRODUCTION

"Mirror, mirror on the wall, who is the fairest of them all?" asked the queen in the fairy tale. Then the magic mirror would respond to her with an honest answer. In reality, wouldn't it be nice if we all have a magic mirror that can tell us all the answers we want?

For those of us who need to know about how to market our businesses but lack the knowledge and experience, a magic mirror would be perfect for us every time we have questions. Unfortunately, this mirror does not exist in real life. That is why we have created this book to help, inform, and educate you like a magic mirror, and hence, we name our book the "Magic Mirror Marketing: A Practical Guide To Business Marketing."

In this book, we'll show you different elements, concepts, and strategies of business marketing that have proven to work well for us and our clients in the past. To start off, we will explain the difference between two types of market demands, which is important to you in determining which marketing strategies you should use. Then we'll go over various types of complete marketing systems you can consider, such as "3 Steps Mastery," "Triple Power," and "3 Growth Pillars." We'll also show what the 3 biggest marketing mistakes you can make and how to avoid them. Later in the book, we'll go into more specific topics, like e-zines, flyers, receipts, events, joint venture, networking, and newsletters. You'll be surprised to see how important and applicable those concepts are in assisting your marketing campaigns when they seem to be unrelated on the surface.

Frankly, business marketing is more than just advertising your products and services in print or online; you have to do a lot more work behind the scene in order to make your campaign more effective. But of course, the more educated and prepared you are, the easier your marketing effort will be. After finishing the book, you will have the knowledge to market your business and achieve the results you want.

As you read, you'll realize that some ideas and topics are presented more than once in the book. The repetition is intentional because, by reading it more than once, the contents will stick better in your mind so you can learn more effectively. It's also important to note that some ideas in one chapter may be slightly contradict with some in another chapter. That doesn't mean either one is right or wrong; what we intend to show you is that both opinions are applicable, depending upon the situation. Seeing things from different angles allows you to have a more complete picture of the concepts. As a famous old saying once says, "There are two sides to each coin"; there is always more than one way to do anything, including customer attraction. So learn different sides of an idea, and apply the one you feel comfortable with based on your situation.

Finally, we encourage you to put those knowledge in practice. A lot of people will read something and think, "Yes, I'll do it someday" or "I wish that is applicable to my business" or "It seems too difficult for me to do," etc. So at the end, they just keep thinking about it, finding excuses not to take immediate actions, or procrastinating until who knows when. The truth is, the concepts in this book are applicable to any businesses; they may not apply fully to your business in particular, but definitely to some extents. What you need to do is to understand the knowledge presented, figure out way that works for you, implement it, and continuously adjust your strategies as your situation evolves. The only way to make things work is by actually trying it out instead of just thinking about it.

If you need further assistance or more information, please let us know so we can offer you more help. That's what we're here for!

.

CHAPTER 1

UNDERSTAND THE "DEMAND" OF MARKET

Marketing is an interesting field because an effective marketing campaign can change people's perception and reaction on the thing that is being advertised and motivate them to take action. But before we talk about marketing from advertiser's perspective, let's understand more about the public's side of marketing – specifically, the "demand" of the market.

For any product or service, marketing capitalizes on two different types of demand – "existing" demand and "created" demand.

Existing demand happens when people are actively looking for a product or service. They know they want it, and have already determined that they will buy it without hesitation. The only question is who they will buy it from. For example, when you travel somewhere for vacation and you know you want to rent a car to drive around town to have more

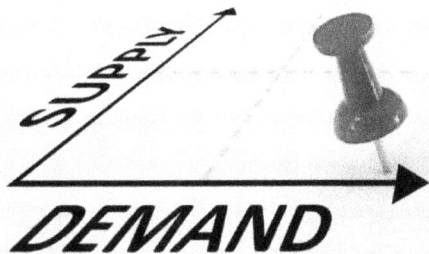

freedom and mobility, your question then isn't about whether you need a rental car or not; it's about which company you want to rent from.

In contrast, created demand occurs when you try to sell a product or service to a market where people either aren't aware of it, or don't know if they need or want it. For instance, when Apple's first launched its iPad in 2010, the whole concept of using a hand-held computer called tablet was new to the general public. Although the product reviews were quite positive, at that time many consumers were not sure why they would need a tablet when they could have used their laptops and smartphones, which were already popular. Some even mocked the name iPad by comparing it to some women's hygiene products. However, once the popularity of iPad was stirred up by the most hard-core Apple fans, and people started to see how a tablet fit in between a laptop and a smartphone, people suddenly felt like they "need" it; the demand for iPad soared ever since.

Unfortunately, many marketers never address this key difference; most of them sell to both existing demand and created demand customers using the same strategy. In reality, the approach you take to sell to someone who already knows what they want should be completely different from that to a person who aren't quite sure what they want or who you are.

Why should you do that? Because you want to get them to the buying decision as quickly as possible. Nowadays, with our technological advancement, consumers are flooded with too many choices and too much information. Many businesses mistakenly extend their selling cycle, or even lose sales, by providing unnecessary details in which consumers might find it irrelevant and lose interest. A thorough selling job in your ad is needed to convince your prospects, but too much unrelated information will cost you sales. You need to avoid that mistake and strike for a balance. That's why you should create two different approaches for two different types of demands. You'll need to tailor the content of your ad by including something and excluding other things in a given targeted market.

How can you make two different campaigns, so that when someone is googling for your service online, they will see exactly what they want to see? Nowadays, setting up a website is so inexpensive that you should have at least two websites; one for people who are looking for your product or service, and one for those who don't know they need you yet.

Let's look at an example to illustrate the difference. Imagine you are selling violin instruction. With one group of customers, they already know they want to learn how to play violin, and they are currently looking for a teacher in a certain area. So when you set up your website or create an ad, you need to answer their main question, "I know I want it, why should I choose you?" Now, with another group of customers, they aren't necessarily looking for your service, as the thought of learning violin may not even cross their minds. Hence, your online or ad campaign should first convince them why they need your service, and then why they should take it from you.

You'll do the same thing with pricing too. The existing demand clients may already have a rough idea of how much it would cost for the violin lessons they are looking for. So you should price competitively. And if you offer extra benefits or values to them than your competitors, you can ask for a premium price. The created demand customer may not know what prices should be. You should first educate them with comparables outside your industry, or show them a scheme of building up value that is not necessary with existing demand customers.

The bottom line is, existing demand customers know exactly what they want, so it would make sense to keep your message short and sweet for them. If you bring in unnecessary information, you'll be jeopardizing your sales. That's why you should always think of who you're selling to first, and then decide what you should tell them about your product or service.

As you've already seen, we strongly suggest using multiple websites for generating leads and tracking. This tactic doesn't cost a fortune, which is great for any business, even for conventional, small, mom-and-pop type of business. Also, with today's technology, you can even do it yourself with website designing and posting without having a computer science university degree!

It is very difficult to have one website show up high on Google for 30 different items. That's why you should pick only 5 or 6 of your most demanded requests and make a site to selling them specifically. The key is to stay focus on those things, and not try to pack 30+ great things about your business into one site.

However, don't be fooled that online campaign is all you need for your business marketing; that's a huge mistake because the internet has screwed up tracking ads for most business. It's true that most business prospects go online and find you 50-85% of the time before they will contact you for more information. But here is an important misconception: if you ask your prospects how they found you, many would say "internet" when, in reality, they received a flyer or pamphlet on hand first, and then went and checked out your website later. Many marketers may think that offline, physical marketing doesn't work anymore because everyone is so used to google things online now. And many small businesses will spend thousands of dollars per year on good old traditional marketing (e.g. physical prints and newspapers), but then is unwilling to spend a few hundred dollars per year on a simple web site to see how many people are actually responding. Both are wrong!

Online and offline campaigns actually complement, not substitute for, each other. When you want to track response rate, you can attach one website to one specific ad source. For example, if you advertise in the Yellow Pages, then dedicate one website just for the Yellow Pages. If you place an ad in a business/trade magazine, then put a different website address in that magazine. Setting up multiple websites may seem like a small step, but it's crucial in helping you track and sell better.

CHAPTER 2

THE "3 STEPS MASTERY"

MARKETING SYSTEM

One factor that all successful businesses and entrepreneurial endeavours have in common is good marketing and advertising strategies. The key to create an effective – and impressive – marketing campaign is to understand and follow the marketing rules and basics, keep them simple, and find ways to apply to and test in your business, with a little bit of your own creativity of course. After you have mastered the core principles, you can then move from industry to industry and achieve exceptional levels of success with those same principles.

In reality, many business owners have no clue about advertising and marketing. They usually copy what their competitors do, which is the worst thing you can do. Why? Because not only is there a chance that your competitors themselves may not know what effective marketing is, it's also possible that what

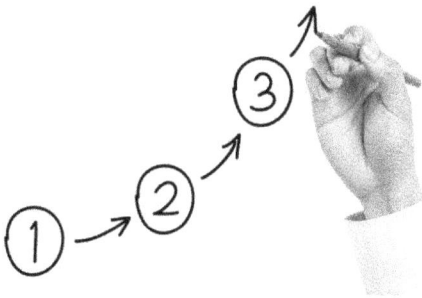

works for them may not work for you. So copying someone is never a good idea.

In this chapter, we will explore a "3 Steps Mastery" marketing system that can help you attract as many clients as you can handle and improve your cash flow. But first, let's understand the rules and principles of marketing and see how they're set the foundation of our mastery marketing system.

RULES AND PRINCIPLES OF MARKETING

There are 9 important rules and 3 fundamental principles that set the stage for our marketing system. Here are the 9 rules:

1) Rule #1 is the most important rule of all. You should realize that the purpose of your entire marketing campaign is NOT to showcase your brand, company name, or creative logo. The ONLY thing that truly matters is to have marketing make money for you.

2) Believe or not, branding can and will happen naturally as result of profitable growth. That's why the focus of your marketing efforts should be on making money instead.

3) Every piece of your advertisement should contain an offer. The offer doesn't necessarily means that you always ask them to buy something from you; you can simply direct them to take some kind of action, like visiting a web page to get something for free.

4) Each of your marketing campaigns should consist of at least 3 steps in order to call it a properly designed campaign. In other words,

when communicating with your current and prospective clients, you must send them a minimum of 3 different pieces.

5) Avoid using any fancy or vague one-liners that say and do nothing to help you make money, which is rule #1.

6) Your personality is actually is your greatest asset in marketing. You should show the world that you are a real live person. A lot of business owners only showcase their businesses, and more often they try to boast the reputation of their company by pretending to be big in size. Putting your face and personality front and center in all your marketing will get you more sales than anything else you do.

7) If your advertising is effective, it should be able to stop your target customers from whatever they are doing and literally compel them to read your ad.

8) If your advertising is effective, it should never look like an advertisement at all.

9) For your advertising to be effective, it should always contain some sort of tracking system so that you know exactly what works or doesn't work.

Besides those 9 rules of marketing, you'll also need to keep in mind the 3 foundational marketing principles that have helped our clients generate huge profits in the past:

1) Focus on generating leads, not sales

2) Use systems to convert leads into sales, and then turn sales into repeat buyers

3)   Use marketing with a measuring system in everything you do

PUTTING THEM TOGETHER

Now let's see how we incorporate all the rules and concepts together into our 3-steps marketing master plan.

Step 1: Generating Leads Instead of Sales

One of the biggest mistakes many entrepreneurs make in their marketing is that they are moving in way too fast for the kill. Treat marketing like dating; the very first thing you focus on should not be getting your girl back to your place into your bed. You should warm her up to you with your personality, sense of humour, or whatever charm you have. They need to know you and trust you first. Only then can you move on to other things. The idea is simple – no interest, no trust, no talk, no deal.

To start generating leads, the FIRST thing you need to do is to find your ideal client. Here you should ask yourself, "Who are you selling to?" Many entrepreneurs have never thought about this question thoroughly. One of the most common responses we've heard is, "I want to sell to anyone with money!" That's so WRONG! When you sell to anyone, you actually sell to no one. So the more focused you can identify in your target client profile, the greater your chance of sales success will be.

Who is your ideal client? The more specific you are, the better this marketing will work. Otherwise, it will be useless. Start jotting down anything you can think of about them. For example:

• How old are they?

- What are their occupations? In what industry?

- What are their income levels?

- What type of vehicles do they drive?

- What kind of clothes they wear after work?

- Are they married?

- How many kids (if any)?

- What are their hobbies?

- What are their dreams, goals, passions, or ambitions?

- What types of books or materials do they usually read?

- What do they usually look for in businesses they buy from? For products, convenience, price?

Now turn all the above answers into an introductory speech from their perspective. Write it in a way as if they are introducing themselves and telling you about their family, lifestyle, interests, and dreams. More importantly, emphasize what kind of problems they are facing, and what solutions you may be able to provide. During the process, try to put a name and a face to your perfect clients and picture them to be very personal, which they should be in real life. Here is an example:

"Hi, my name is (name of your ideal client), I'm ……. years old. I work as a/an ……. (details about them)"

And then turn this into a WANTED poster ad like the example below. You can put this in front of you any time you write a new ad, as if you're addressing JUST to that person. With this exercise, your ads will shine more and will be written to the person you should be selling to.

WANTED

[Insert details of who they are and what they look for from career, life, business, etc.]

If you, or anyone you know, fit this description, please contact [your name] immediately at [your phone number with area code], or through [name@yourdomain.com] to receive your FREE *The 3-Steps Formula To Grow Your Business* [or whatever you want to offer].
No catch, just FREE help to grow your business.

Your next task is to create an ad. In the following example, you will see an ad that worked really well in the past. You can use that as a sample template for creating your own lead generation system.

To make those ads, think about what would attract them to your business for the first time. If they are looking for more information first, then a booklet or a pamphlet would be an appropriate tool to use to lure them in.

Perhaps they are seeking some free small gadgets when they visit your site or store. Your job is to find something that they would want, and give it to them just for coming in or expressing their interest. When you know who you are marketing to, their needs will become apparent.

Begin collecting newspapers, magazines, or publications that you think your target clients are reading. Take note of the types of articles that run in those materials. You would want your lead generating ad to look as much like an article as possible; editorial style ads generate as many as 6 times of viewers as traditional ads.

What information do you think is most useful to your prospects? What would be most interesting to them? Start working on a 1-3 page special report you can offer your prospects for lead generation. For instance, you can write about "The Most Recent Industry Trends That Can Help You _____," or "The 5 Most Important Tips For Improving Your _____ Business."

Pay attention to a few key points about the ad:

- Your company name is not in your headline. Be honest, your prospects isn't going to care about how creative your company name is; what they are most eager to learn is how you can help solve their problems.

- Differentiate yourself from all other ads in the Yellow Pages or Kijiji that look and sound similar by saying, "Hey! Before you call any of these other guys – you had better read this one first." And if you make it looks like a newsworthy article, wouldn't you want to read it too?

- You make it look like an article because it gets 7 times as many readers as advertisements.

- You are a raising question in your ad that is often overlooked by people, but is very important to them to ponder.

- You are giving them a time limit in order to create an urgency for them to take action.

- Note that you have included a testimonial, with an actual person's name and location. You're making your ad unique by offering PROOF of success via your past client's mouth.

- Note you're also offering your prospects an education of the topic. They can learn about roofing – what they should and should not do before they make a decision on who they are going to hire.

At this point, you must be able to deliver to them the freebies or bonuses that you promise, and there should be no catch for them to collect as indicated. Essentially, what we are doing here is to attract your target clients by saying "here we are, we have something you may find interesting, and we will give it to you for free." This allows you to collect their contact information for building a database of your prospects. Once you've built one, USE IT!

Some good rules in making lead generations and follow-up letters:

- You need to have a good headline. You can use either an attention-grabbing based or benefit based headline. For instance, "Warning! Stop! If you are about to…" or "The Fastest and Easiest Way To … – For FREE!" or "Afraid of … ? Let me tell you how to … ," or "How To Win Over Friends And Influence People." It would be even better if you make the headline in a different font from the rest of the ad. You can use all bold, but NOT all caps because it is difficult to read, and it gives out an impression that you're yelling at them. Visually, your ad must stand out from all other ads in the section. When you look at the section where your ad will be posted, you can get a feeling of what all other ads generally look like, so you can contrast with the others in the section.

- Your ad should address the readers – not yourself. Its focus is to tell about how you can help them, not boast about how great you can to do with certain job. Talk with them like a "conversation in a normal way" instead of "advertising in a business way"; think of it like you are talking with a prospect for the first time and you try to get their attention. Also, to give your ad a more personalized feeling, you should write your ad as if you are talking to just one single person at a time. Most ads are written as if they are broadcasting to a group of audience, which makes it sound more distant and that's not good. Use words like "you" and "yours." At the end, count the words "you" and "yours" versus "I" and "we" – the "I," "me," or "we" should be less than 5% of all words.

- Always address the benefits, NOT the features, of your product or service to them. Imagine this: after you tell them everything about yourself, your company, and your product or service, they ask you,

"So what?" Then how would you respond? That's why you should tell them what your capability actually means to them, and what values will be transferred to them when they read your ad and call you; simply showcasing your business is never a good idea.

- Leave them with a good emotion as they read your ad. Help them picture in their head their new lifestyle after they use your product or service and enjoy its benefits, thinking how glad they are with what you offer.

- The biggest mistake many people made is to not include a call to action. You MUST place one in your ad. An action could be requesting your report, getting their free coupons, or booking a free consultation. Make it a limited time offer or a limited quantity to motivate them further.

Step 2: Turning Your Leads Into Sales

You may have generated great leads from step 1, but unless you have a solid follow-up system in place, you won't convert as many leads as you hope for. That's why it's important to write, test, and improve your follow-up letters, and then send them out as often as possible, well, at least 3 times.

Imagine, if your first letter converts 10% of your prospects into buyers, the second letter converts 5% and third letter converts 3%, you will have converted 18% of your prospects to paid clients. The letters can do all the work and you don't even need to have a single meeting or a phone call. Sounds great, doesn't it?

Once you've used this ad system for some time, you will get an idea of how much money you can make every month when you send out a certain number of letters. So, from this exercise, your goal is to build yourself a business system that can make you money on a regular basis, and can be repeated, grown, or shrunk based on your business needs.

The most common way to follow up with your prospects is through direct mails (i.e. letters) as we discussed. There are other effective channels as well, such as emails, audio clips, and videos. After they have expressed their interest in your offer, you take down their contact information and send them the free gifts. But eventually, you need to get them to buy into your products and services. The 3-steps follow-up campaign is then used to close the deal.

In order for the campaign to work well, you need to include 4 key factors into your success formula:

1) **Attention** – You need to get them to read your ad right from the start. Your headline is the KEY to whether your follow-up will make or break the deal. If you want to get an idea of what a good headlines look like, you can actually find them in magazines like Cosmopolitan Magazine! They have some of the best headline writers in the world, so you should pay attention to how they write their cover headlines.

2) **Interest** – You must make them stop whatever they are doing and read your letter. You need to build up their interest and show them

you have something that they will want. If you have done your research and targeted the right person, you would know what they are interested in.

3) **Desire** – This is where you introduce them to the most fabulous offer they have ever seen. We usually like to bundle various products or services together and offer them as one incredible deal that they can't refuse. Name the bundle something different from your competitors so your prospects can't compare apples to apples. Also offer them a guarantee, or a price plan, and, more importantly, testimonials from your past happy clients, which can prove that you have delivered on your promises to others.

4) **Action** – This is the most important, yet often neglected, step in the entire marketing campaign. You need to ask them to take action NOW. Give them every possible reason to trust you, and incentives to visit your store and buy from you right now. On the flip side, you should also make them understand what will miss out if they don't take action.

Step 3: Testing And Measuring

As we mentioned before, effective marketing requires you to try various things and track whatever you do. Eventually, you will be able to figure out what is effective in serving your promotional needs. Here are some examples you can test for your ad:

- Different ad headlines

- One-pager vs. multiple page letter

- Styles in opening paragraph

- Different font

- Font size

- Font color (black & white vs. color)

- Signature in blue vs. black ink

- Deadlines vs. no deadlines for taking actions

- Free samples vs. none

- Quantity discounts

- Bonus bundle

- Method of payments (cash, cheque, credit card, payment instalments)

- Method of response (phone, fax, mail, email, in-store visit)

- Usual white envelope vs. color envelope

- Teaser copy on envelope vs. none

- Actual stamp vs. pre-printed postage

When you test, make sure you only test one thing at a time, or the test will become invalid. If you test two things at the same time and you see a difference in response rate, you won't be able to tell which variable actually causes this difference. For the same reason, your test must be run in the same list or publication as it was initially, so that you can have a direct comparison of your test variables in the same setting.

One advice about getting feedbacks: NEVER ask your family, friends, or co-workers for their impressions on your marketing! Due to their relationships with you, you often can't get an honest, objective opinion; they either don't want to say anything bad to hurt your feeling when your ad really sucks, or they will try to pressure their opinions on you without hesitation because they think you guys are so close that you should accept everything they say. That's why you should either hire a professional to develop a campaign template as a foundation, or do it yourself with the suggestions listed here and actually test campaign to see the real results.

Once your testing is done, you need to have a way to measure its effectiveness. An easy way to keep track is to make a simple excel spreadsheet record, and write down exactly what you did, how long you did it, what the outcomes are, and how well it worked or didn't. Then with those results, you rank them on a scale of 1 (winners) to 4 (losers):

1 – Fantastic; it brought you lots of sales, new leads, or positive comments from your customers and prospects

2 – Marginal; it got you break even (or made a small profit), or some new leads or positive comments

3 – Failing; it made you lose money or time and gain nothing in return; no new leads or sales, no one even noticed your ad

4 – Disastrous; it was a big loser; you received nothing but negative feedback and comments, and completely wasted your time

You would handle each of those categories differently. You would definitely run the 1's again and again. If you have a campaign that works for you like a charm, why stop it? Don't stop just because you are tired of it, keep going! Send it out to every new lead that comes in your way. If it worked in the past, it will work again. You'll then test the 2's again and hope they will work better this time. With the 3's and 4's, you will hold off for now and try them again in 6 to 12 months as the environment may change more favourably later on. Sometimes, what doesn't work now may work well in a few months because the internet and world are constantly changing. That's why you never throw out any of your test methods and results. Of course, you may also need to modify them accordingly to fit the new conditions better.

Besides categorizing your results from 1 to 4, you can even add personal thoughts on why some things worked or didn't. These notes you make could become invaluable to you in 6 to 12 months because you can refer back to them when it's time for more strategies. Rather than reinventing the wheel, you may realize that you've already tested it but simply forgot if it did or didn't work.

You can also write out how you can improve them, such as more fun and exciting, more profitable and enticing to prospects, more appealing to their emotions, etc. Basically, write down anything you can think of to make it better! Then keep these types of results and comments in a marketing binder on a regular basis and review them monthly or whenever you need new promotion ideas.

So there you have the principle of writing and testing a direct response campaign. Once you find a winner, keep using it as many times and often as you can until it doesn't work anymore. If you have not yet found a winning method, don't worry and keep trying new ideas.

CHAPTER 3

THE "TRIPLE POWER" MARKETING PLAN

Many people dream of starting their own businesses and becoming their own bosses. But most people don't start mainly because they fear of failing. In reality, anyone "could" succeed in any kind of business if only they knew how to keep their businesses away from failing, which in turn would overcome their fear.

Now how can they make their business fail-proof? The answer: knowledge. It is so important because it empowers people with the ability to handle problems and avoid pitfalls. In our discussion of marketing, the key knowledge required is to know how to target your audience, how to promote your business, and how to sell your brand and product/service. If entrepreneurs have these key pieces of knowledge, which we'll call it "Triple Power" marketing, the failure rate with their start-ups or established businesses would drop.

TRIPLE POWER COMPONENTS

So what exactly is "Triple Power" marketing plan? It is a combination of organic, guerrilla, and attraction marketing to promote your business.

1. Organic Marketing

This is a cultivating approach in which you advertise and grow your sales through your current customers and networks. You need to go beyond referral requests, and instead ask for a full introduction to anyone they know who would benefit in the same way like they have from doing business with you.

The beauty of this approach is that it allows you to avoid the stress of old fashion hard-selling and the traditional expensive advertising. More importantly, you're not waiting passively and hoping that one day a customer will mention your name and service to his/her friend who may need you; you're constantly asking for new clients to talk and explain benefits to.

A full introduction is critical because even if you are given with a referral's phone number or email, when you contact them without any prior introduction, you're still making an unsolicited sales call. Worst, the person on the line most likely will react with suspicion. You think the sales would succeed? I don't think so. That's why referrals are so uncomfortable for everyone involved. But when you deal with new clients who have already been told about the wonderful work you do and the benefits you can provide them, and you call them only when they want to be called, everyone involved would become more relaxing, and sales would be much easier. That's the key component of organic marketing.

However, there is a real danger with it; you may need to get close, probably uncomfortably close for some, to your customers in order to gain enough trust from them and have them do the introduction for you.

2. Guerrilla Marketing

Guerilla | Gorilla

LIKE A SOLDIER

LIKE A BIG MONKEY (OR KING KONG!)

This is an advertising strategic concept where businesses promote their products or services in a non-traditional, fast-acting, and inexpensive way. The main point of guerrilla marketing is that advertising are done exclusively on streets or public places like shopping malls, parks, or beaches with maximum client traffic, so that you can attract a bigger audience. It's like guerrilla warfare, where small groups of soldiers would show up in a short period of time here and there, causing damages and causalities. Now you know why this form of marketing is called guerrilla marketing.

This marketing strategy is especially helpful in turning around a company that is in a downhill emergency, such as needing to come up with a million dollar sales within the next 30 minutes. Let us give you an example. Many,

many years ago, one of the housing developing businesses in Ontario had problems selling their new houses in a newly developed rural area. There was no traffic, no sales, and nobody even knew they existed. The company would go down fast if they had no sales within a month. However, suggestions were made to hang price tags from the chimney (4x8-foot plywood price tags from chimney and on porches everywhere, with the old prices crossed out, and the new prices in huge number). They were also advised to park a moving van, with a 30-foot banner across it, on the highway that ran past the development site. Then they put up many hand-made posters everywhere that said "buy direct from the builder." Together with a few other guerrilla strategies, all of their units were sold out within the next few months.

3. Attraction Marketing

While it may be overwhelming for some people, this is a safe and comfortable approach for many people to attract, grow, and sustain their businesses by doing relatively easy and inexpensive activities, such as public speaking, publishing blog or newsletters, hosting educational sessions for current and prospective clients. Now you may be wondering, "What do those have to do with marketing?" Well, you want to position yourself as 'the expert' in your marketplace by sharing your knowledge, so that prospects will come to you, instead of you going after them. The essence of this form of marketing is, "If I call you, I'm a salesman. If you call me, I'm an expert." Of course, you still need to sell

during the whole process, but it would be much easier to close the deal when the prospects know your worth and call you first.

So is there any problem in this strategy? Definitely! In order to position yourself as the expert, you must already be (or soon become) a genuine expert. That means you need to stay at the edge of your industry's trend, or to be (or already become) a walking encyclopaedia of every single thing related to your field, so you can let everyone knows that you're indeed the go-to person in your network. Here is an example. John is a wine lover, and he is good at designing and building high quality wine cellars for homes and restaurants. But when he first started his own business in the field, nobody knew of him and he had no phone call whatsoever. Later, he got some suggestions that helped lift him off the ground. First, he hosted a series of wine and cheese receptions at his brand new wine tasting room for builders, architects, and interior designers, so that those individuals could come through the door and see the quality of his work while enjoying his wine. Not only would those receptions position him as an expert in wine and wine cellar construction business , they would also give him a chance for ice-breaking when he went out to physically meet and deliver invitations to builders and general contractors at building sites. Then, he was able to build a client database when he phoned his targeted audience, asking for contact information (e.g. names, email addresses) that he should send his invitations to. All approaches together got him business calls and sales conversations that he didn't have before, even in economic downturn.

The above "Triple Power" marketing strategies can help any business to succeed against any odds in any kind of economy, as you are taking risks of failing in order to become different and attractive to your clients, while your competitors are taking cover and trying to play safe and conventional. You can succeed by taking market shares from those who don't use it.

CHAPTER 4

THE "3 GROWTH PILLARS"
IN BUSINESS

Whether you're in business for profits, career challenge, personal satisfaction, or what have you, you want to, and need to, grow it in order to keep it going. Even maintaining status quo is a form of growth in that you need to replenish your client pool with new ones as quickly as you're losing your old ones.

There are 3 ways any business can grow (i.e. the 3 growth pillars):

1) Get more customers to come in and visit

2) Get them to purchase more from you each time

3) Get them to purchase from you more frequently

WHAT EXACTLY ARE THE 3 PILLARS?

The idea sounds simple and intuitive, but doing it may not be as straight-forward. Let's look at each one in detail.

1. Get More Customers

Usually, attracting more customers to our door is the first option that will come to our mind when it comes to growth in business and profits. After all, all businesses need a steady flow of customers/clients in order to stay healthy. This strategy is very important, but it's also quite costly and labour intensive. And remember, each of the 3 growth pillars is equally important and we should give equal consideration. So unless your business is completely brand new, you shouldn't focus your time and energy on new customer attraction. In other chapters of this book, we'll examine different ways in how to get new customer, so now let's look at the other 2 pillars for business growth.

2. Get Them To Purchase More From You Each Time

Once someone has come in your door and decided to buy from you, you've already overcome the biggest sales hurdle, which is to get them to notice you and take action. But then you need to keep going with your thought and effort, so that you can increase the value and profit from each transaction.

I recently had a similar shopping experience at a Coach outlet store in Calgary. They got me in the "buying" mood because I knew ahead of time that everything in the store was 50% off. That was a crazy deal I couldn't pass! However, instead of just one item as originally planned, I ended up buying 3 items, as they had extra 20% off (on top of 50%) on selected items. So at the end, Coach had me bought more than I expected. As you see, getting customers to your door and in a buying mood is the hardest part of sales, but getting them to buy more during their stay is relatively easy. All you need to do is to give them a good reason to spend more by providing them with additional incentives and values.

Now the question is, how can you apply this concept to your own business? Think, can you add more of your products or services and super-size them while keeping at the same price? Or bundle up various items and sell it at a discount or as a value pack? For example, every item you see and buy in Costco comes in super-size or bulk package, nothing small. In fact, Costco has built an entire business based on this idea.

And how about offering different levels of your items/services at different prices? With higher price, each level can offer more perks. You may probably wonder if increasing price would turn people off. Well, in any customer base, you'll always have a group of people who doesn't mind paying higher price because they want best of the best in everything, for premium quality, prestigious status, convenience, or whatever reasons. Why do you think car makers can sell both luxury and economy models at any given time and in any economic condition? And how can airlines sell both first class and economy class in every plane? That's because different price for different people with different needs.

Regardless of what kind of business you're in, you can always find a way to upgrade your products and services, and get your clients/customers to buy more from you. For example, a financial planner can offer insurance products to clients besides investment products.

3. Get Them To Purchase From You More Frequently

Imagine you successfully got your customers to your door, and they spent more money after you offered them more values at higher prices. Once you've got the transaction that you worked hard for. Is that the end for their value to you? Of course not! Your next step is to get them to return and buy from you more often. It's easier and less expensive to have an existing customer to come back and buy again than to attract another new one to you to make a purchase. They've already established a business relationship and – hopefully – had an enjoyable experience with you, so you don't need to work as hard in attraction, ice-breaking, and persuasion anymore for their subsequent purchase.

And yet, many businesses fail to put enough attention and effort in keeping their existing customers, let alone getting another transaction from them. One possible reason is that they assume those customers will automatically return for more when they have the same needs, since they were presumably happy with their past business experience. But that's a very dangerous assumption, leading to lack of efforts and eventual closing of the business. Let's be honest to yourself: how loyal are you to businesses that you usually shop at, like a cellphone provider or grocery store? Right now, if a competitor comes and offers you a deal that is cheaper or more convenient than your current choice, how willing would you be to give this new vendor a try and switch over? Most likely yes!

In fact, there's probably only 1 or 2 businesses that you'll ever stick to in your entire life, such as your family doctor and dentist, and it may be due to the personal trust and relationships that you've established with them previously. Otherwise, you may switch it over too. Now, try to relate that same thinking to your customers, and you can imagine how replaceable you are to them.

However, with strategies and efforts, it's possible for you to change their perception and keep them on your side. Here are 3 suggestions:

1) **Keep in contact with your customers more often** – With frequent communication, you're getting yourself "face time" to your clients so you'll always be fresh in their mind. There are many ways to stay in touch. While the following list of suggestions is not exhaustive, you should incorporate a variety of them, depending on the size of your group. For example, you should use the top methods if you have a small group of clients and you're comfortable in executing them (in terms of workload, travel, time commitment, etc.). However, if you have a large number of clients, you may have to use

the suggestions towards the end of the list as the top few ones may not be practical to carry out.

- Meetings (you go visit them)

- Meetings (invite them to visit you)

- Phone calls (you call them)

- Phone calls (your assistant calls them)

- Letters from you (not typed and printed, but hand-written)

- Letters from your assistant (could be typed and printed)

- Special occasion notes/cards (e.g. birthdays, anniversaries, holidays)

- Regular monthly newsletter sent by mail

- Special offers sent by mail

- Mass emails

- Mass faxes

2) **Treat your select customers like VIP** – In order to connect better with those customers who have been in business with your business frequently or for a long time, you should treat them differently from those who are new or have done business with you just once or twice. By giving your preferred customers the VIP treatment, such as priority in sales, special deals, and loyalty discount, you show them how much you appreciate their support to you.

3) **Enrol them in an ongoing/loyalty program instead of letting them go after a one-time sale** – An ongoing/loyalty program is one of the best ways to keep your customers because you're giving them an incentive (e.g. rewards) to return to you again and again. Having steady customer flows is a wonderful way to keep your business stable so you're not suffering from "feast or famine" cycle.

To create your loyalty package, you first need to determine the proper amount of your products or service your clients would receive, at what price and how often they would receive it. For example, let's say you start a company shovelling snow for residents or businesses in winter time. Normally, you get a call from them, go and do the job, get paid, and that is the end of the transaction. You will then wait for the next call for the next job and the next paycheque, and this cycle continues. If you get no call, then you'll have no job and no pay. That will become "feast or famine" for your business. However, you can avoid this problem by creating an ongoing service program for your customers. Let's say each service is priced at $100 and for each customer you have 24 services in one winter session (one service per week for 6 months, from October to March). Instead of getting all $2,400 in 6 months, you can create an annual program by dividing the amount by 12 so you can get a consistent income of $200 per month. You will then approach your customers with this offer, saying that with this monthly plan, jobs will get done automatically as soon as snow starts to fall, no hassle, no worries. From clients' perspective, it will be convenient for them to have everything taken care of without reminders, and they won't be hit with a bigger payment every time they receive your service. As for your business, not only is your cash flow more steady now, and you can also plan your work schedule ahead of time since you now know how many clients (jobs) you'll have to do. Better yet, if you get your new customers to sign up with the ongoing plan, your schedule will fill up quick, and you can then cut down on your advertising cost and effort.

The ongoing/loyalty program works for almost any type of business; all you need is a little creativity that fits your particular business resources and needs.

So unless you just start a brand new business without any customers, you should seriously consider how to integrate the last two pillars of business growth; it's cheaper, more effective, and profitable for you to focus on maximizing your current client base than to lure new ones to your door.

CHAPTER 5

HOW TO AVOID THE 3 BIGGEST MARKETING MISTAKES

Many small business owners, entrepreneurs, and professionals have no problem in delivering their product or service to their customers. But many of them don't know how to properly get the words out about their businesses to attract people, and they make costly mistakes in their marketing campaigns.

WHAT ARE THE 3 BIGGEST ONES?

Of all the mistakes, we will discuss the worst 3 and some suggestions on how to avoid them.

Mistake #1: Always Hunt For New Clients But Forget About The Old Ones

This is by far the biggest mistake of all. Remember previously we talked about 3 ways to grow any business:

1) Get more customers

2) Get them to buy more from you each time

3) Get them to purchase from you more frequently

For many new business owners who don't have a single customer, it would make sense to grow their businesses by keep getting new clients. However, if you've already established some client base, this method may not be that effective because it can be time, energy and money consuming. Why? Because you have to get their attention (advertisement), make yourself appealing to them (unique selling proposition), give them attention and gifts (discounts, bonuses, offers), convince them that you are the perfect choice for them (guarantees, warranties, testimonials, etc.), and then make the sale (seal the deal). Some say it can be 5-7 times more costly to get a new customer to buy from you than to have an old one buying from you. I do believe it! And more importantly, while they focus on attracting new customers and new deals, they often forget about the existing ones they already gained, let alone maximizing the value of them. As human nature goes, those customers may subconsciously resent the fact that they aren't being appreciated as much after the initial sale.

Now as a savvy marketer, you would still work hard attracting your customers at the beginning. But instead of forgetting about them after the initial sale, you would bring them into your business family by engaging with them. Instead of having just a one-time customer at a time, you now have many customers to choose from, and have the opportunity to sell them as often as you like.

Being a good marketer, having an established client base wouldn't stop you from looking for more customers; it just wouldn't be the entire focus of your effort. And while you pursue a new prospect, you would be much more relaxed in doing it, as business needs are more than covered by all of the current customers. You would definitely not appear as desperate. Ever heard of a saying "Needy is creepy"? Most of us don't like "needy" people because they give off that desperate vibe.

Solutions To Mistake #1:

1) **You need to have a good customer database** – Many small business owners don't keep track of any (or enough) demographic information about their customers. Even if you already have a good database, you need to maximize the use of it. Otherwise, there is no point of keep collecting information. So if you haven't had a database, the first thing to do is, of course, to make one by filling it with as many of your customer details as possible. For certain businesses, such as physicians, insurance agents, or financial planners, they tend to create such a database naturally, since collecting those information is part of their process of doing business. But with other businesses, like grocery stores and restaurants where customers don't really need to disclose any information, building a database may be more challenging. What should you do to get their contact information? Instead of making disclosure mandatory when they make their purchases, it would be better to find

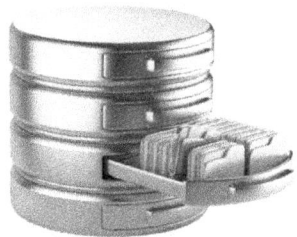

ways to make them WANT to give you their information – by means of "ethical bribing." Here are ways that are proven to work effectively, for example:

- Create a membership club with exclusive newsletters, insights, recipes, benefits, etc.

- Send out (regular mail or email) discount codes or coupons

- Make a draw for free products, services, etc.

2) **Communicate a lot more often with your past and current customers** – Once you've built a database, you'll need to use it. Otherwise, it'll just be a waste of your effort. The marketing purpose of this database is for you to communicate with all your customers on a regular basis. There are different opinions as to how often is considered "regular," but in our viewpoint, communication should be at least once a month. Especially for a new business, if you really want to start engaging with your customers and get the ball going, we would even suggest once a week. Let's say you send one email per week and one physical mail per month to all you clients. Then you'll have a total of about 64 (= 52 + 12) "touch points" per year. Does that seem like a lot? Well, it depends. If you make them all sales-focused, then yes, it'll be way too much for anyone to handle; it'll feel pushy. But if you mix it up with some newsletters or stories, then no, it won't be

overwhelming. So, you need to focus on more than just selling, and avoid being too "salesy."

On one hand, keep them fun and light. Tell your clients fun facts about you and your staff, and stories about your business. You can also include things that aren't necessarily related to your business like joke of the week, funny cartoons, cooking recipes, etc. On the other hand, use them to promote feature products or services, as well as provide information on special events or sales, or weekly tip about your area of expertise. The idea of communication is to build up a relationship (and giving yourself "face time") over time with your customers, so that they are more familiar with you and your business when it comes to sale time. You would want them to look forward to receiving your newsletters, and miss it if they don't. If they start to complaint to you when they don't get their regular newsletter from you, or voluntarily give you their new address when they move, you know you are doing a really good job with your communication.

Other than emails and newsletters, you can also send greeting cards for holidays and special occasions, like birthdays, Christmas, etc. Those can be counted in those 64 touch points too. To take a step even further, you may want to contact them over the phone to see how they're doing, or invite them to a "customer appreciation" event. The one concern that people often have in mind when it comes to phone call is the "do-not-call" list because legally you cannot solicit over the phone if people explicitly remove their names on the call list. Be sure to check out the complete information on this regulation, but if your clients have done business with you in the past and they haven't opted out of your subscriber list, you should be okay. If done properly, phone call is a very effective marketing strategy. The bottom line is, you always want to keep yourself in your customers' minds, so that when they do have needs in your type of business, you would become their "first choice."

3) **Always keep your business fresh with "new and improved" campaigns** – Nowadays, virtually any product has a makeover on a regular basis. For example, every year, iPhone and Samsung come out with improved smartphone models, and automobile industry will always advertise on TV and social media with the slogan "the all new 20XX [car name]... blah blah blah." Even boring household items like dishwashing soap, laundry detergent, and paper towel often get modified with new features like ultra-bleach micro-particles, extra absorbing pouches and silk smooth texture, etc. Well-known brand names always spice things up with "new and improved" campaigns in order to keep their customers interested and loyal, so they won't be seduced by competitors. You should do the same for your business too! One of the best ways is to develop various versions of your existing product/service. For

example, if your regular version costs $100 (with a profit margin of $50), then you create a high-priced version with many extras and improvements, and you charge $400 for it (with a higher profit margin of $250).

There are two reasons behind this method. First, it can potentially give you with some very high ticket sales with great profit margins. The reality is, in any customer base, you'll always have some people who are willing to pay top dollars for the very best of everything. So you, instead of your competitors, should take advantage of this demand sector and earn those profits. Second, even if you can't sell a single "deluxe" product of yours, the two versions can create a comparison that makes your regular version look like a real bargain. At the other end of the price spectrum, you can introduce a low-priced version (but still with a profit margin that makes it worthwhile), stripping down any benefits that seem to be non-essential. Just as there are high-end customers in any society, you'll also have people who want to be economical and only buy the bare basics at the lowest price possible. Different variations fit different needs. And the more variety you offer to your customers, the more reasons you can contact them, and the more you can keep them interested in your business.

Mistake #2: Your Marketing Is Boring

In today's digital world, not only do we see advertisement in traditional media, we also see them on social media. Literally, we are all bombarded by thousands of ads every day! Think about print ads in newspapers, magazines, commercials on TV, radio, internet (e.g. YouTube, Facebook), promo products and sampling, bus stop signs, billboards, flyers, direct mails, signage on and in stores, on buses and cars, and even in public bathrooms... the list can go on and on!

Now you know this is the kind of competition your marketing effort is up against in getting people's attention. So you can't afford to be boring; you need to be creative! For big businesses, they tend to focus on "branding," "repetition," and "soft sell" to get their names out there. With a much bigger budget to spend, they can make their ads pretty and visually appealing. But the problem is that it's not easily track-able; it's hard to see how effective or ineffective the marketing campaign is. And with small business like ours, we simply don't have that kind of budget to play with. That's why we always suggest the method that is track-able and accountable, which is direct response marketing.

As marketing guru, Dan Kennedy, says, "You have to repel to attract." Most of us are afraid of offending anyone for the fear of what they might think or say about us. We start off with an unrealistic hope that everyone is, or may become, a potential customer. But the fact is, the tighter you define exactly who your most-desirable and most-avoided customers are, the more focus your effort can be, and the better chance of success you'll have. Also, your ultimate goal in business should be to serve as many customers as you can (or want) and create a phenomenal profit for your efforts in the meantime. Business is all about survival of the fittest. If, during the course of doing your business, you piss off your competitors or some prospects, that's okay. You shouldn't worry about how others think about you; just focus on your own. People who buy your idea will come to you, and if your strategy successfully steals outside clients for you, who cares about what your competitors think?

Solutions To Mistake #2:

First and foremost, you need to remember that not everybody you meet is going to be a warm lead for your business. Most people ask questions simply out of curiosity or politeness. Some will make serious considerations, but eventually only a few will do business with you. This is why you need to take a moment to visualize your ideal customer you want to attract. While this isn't exhaustive, here are factors to consider:

- Gender

- Marriage status

- Age group

- Occupation

- Income level

- Residence location

- Vehicle they drive

- Pet ownership

- Hobbies/interest

- Spending habit

- Reading habit

- TV shows/movies

- Political view/religion

Once you have this ideal customer in your mind, you'll then design one part of marketing message for and address to them specifically. Create the piece as if you're talking to them directly. Now do the same exercise with the type of customers you want to avoid the most. Another part of the marketing message should focus on repelling them. Here is an example:

You'll notice there are extra drawings in the letter. Whether those are "pretty" or not is subject to debate, but they sure get people's attention, and the letter definitely doesn't look ordinary and boring!

Other than drawings, you also need a good tag line, mission statement, or guarantee that can differentiate you from the pack (i.e. good unique selling proposition) and really give your prospects strong reasons to work with you. Let's look at some classic or generic ones that can be found on a phone book and see how boring they are:

- *"Operating and serving [an area] since 1985"* – So what? Knowing the fact that you've been around for decades doesn't say anything about what or how well you can deliver for your product/service. All it tells me is the company is an old-timer.

- *"Products and services from the company you can trust"* – Obviously, as a prospect without any prior experience with the business, would you be convinced to trust a company when someone simply tell you to trust him? I know I won't.

- *"Best pizza and ribs in town"* – Again, best in town based on whose account? Or is it simply self-proclaimed? Am I convinced and excited? I don't think so.

On the other side of the story, let's look at what good tag lines look like:

- *"Fresh, hot pizza delivered to your door in 30 minutes or less... Guaranteed"* – This is an old one from Domino's Pizza, and it's probably the best example we've seen because it gets the major points across quickly and clearly. You have fresh and hot pizza, fast, and guaranteed. They promise you what and how you'll get. The story has it that this slogan helped take them from a college drop-out's start-up to become the leader in their competitive market within 10 years.

- *"Our consultation can help you create at least $15,000.00 in profits, or else it's FREE"* – Notice how this example (and the previous one) include guarantee about their product or service? That's what makes them so powerful.

You may not think you have guarantees, but in reality, you probably do; you just don't know, promote, or use it. Imagine, if a client were truly unsatisfied with your product or service, let you know about it (or even threaten to call the press), would you give them their money back? You probably would. In that case, you do guarantee you workmanship, either willingly or unwillingly. You just never advertise that guarantee. By offering guarantee, you're using a strategy called "risk reversal." Essentially, you're taking all the risks away from your client and putting it on your own shoulders. That will take away one of the biggest obstacles that prospects have about doing business with you, which is the fear that they might get ripped off. With a good guarantee, you will attract customers more easily and you can charge higher prices for that.

Now you may worry that cheating customers will take advantage of your guarantee and rip you off. True, it's very possible that it can happen. But think of it as a cost of doing business. If done right, a good guarantee can attract much more business and profit for you than the money you lose to fulfill your guarantee; we would say that the benefits outweigh risks. Plus, as mentioned before, you can charge higher price to account for those potential losses. But of course, if you're getting a lot of refund requests, then you should seriously consider what is wrong instead; maybe the quality of your product or service isn't up to par (in which you should fix it or do something different), or you're dealing with a bunch of very cheap and fishy clients (in which you should fix your ad to avoid any more wrong customers and try to attract the right ones).

Mistake #3: You Are A Lazy Marketer

What's considered laziness in marketing? When you rely on only one or two marketing media to attract new customers! For example, social media like website, Facebook, or YouTube work best for you, and you only rely on those since then. Logically, you may think keep using your best marketing tools is a good idea. After all, why switch to some other modes of communication (e.g. letters, tradeshows, flyers, doorknob ads) that have yet to show any effectiveness? However, the problem to this thinking is, unless your method(s) definitely captures 100% of your target audience, you should have other methods to capture the untouched portion of audience. Keep in mind that not all other methods will work (or as well as your best ones), but as long as their per-unit costs are within your reasonable parameters, it'll still make economic sense to try them. By adding new tools, you can reach the population that would have been missed by your best methods alone, even if it's just 10%.

Another reason for more variety of marketing media is that you'll never know when your best advertising tool(s) will disappear. I don't mean to sound paranoid, but this is a very real concern. For example, the recent anti-spam regulations prohibit you from solicitation to someone who never explicitly enrols in your contact list, which means you can't do cold-call or cold-fax marketing strategies anymore. The regular snail mail won't work if postal workers are ever on strike. New social media emerge constantly; Facebook and YouTube didn't exist until mid-2000. They are some of the most prominent marketing tools now, but who knows when they will become replaced by something even better. And as online marketing gains popularity, traditional media like newspapers are cutting back staff and expenses, and some of them might go out of business. Therefore, if you depend on only one or two tools, and it no longer exists suddenly, then you'll be in trouble.

The third reason is to help grow a "whole" image for your business. If you are only in one or two spots, you may not seem to be well-known, and that gives out a perception of being small and weak. But if you're advertising in 5, 6, or 10 different ways, you'll become omnipresent, which make you appear to be very strong and stable. Often, people might respond to one type of marketing, but they'll use your other forms of marketing(s) to confirm their decision. For example, they may receive your flyers or doorknob ads, but they will google your business to see how legitimate you are based on the ranking, appearance and content of your website. Previously, we talked about using marketing strategies that is track-able and accountable instead of spending money and doing a flashy branding that produces nothing. But this is the only "branding" you should try to do because, at the end of the day, your customers' psychology and perception matters. Let all your direct response advertising feed each other and grow your business image as a whole.

Solutions To Mistake #3:

So, if you're now depending upon only a few different ways of advertising, it's time to start branching out and trying new and different tools. Once you have carried out a variety of methods, you need to track everything you do, and trust me, it's not that difficult. The first thing is to include a "call to action" in all advertising you do. Along with that, you have to include a different tracking system (e.g. promotion code, phone number, contact name) for each type of ad you do. Let's say you offer 30% discount off your product/service. On your website, you can use a discount code "Web30," and in your newsletter/email you can use "Email30." Or, if you want to rent out your apartment, you can put down your contact name as "Jon" (whatever your first name is) on Kijiji/online ad, and then use "Chris" (your middle name) for your printed classified ad. By using different systems, you can track the cost of each advertising tool, the number of leads it gets, and the number of sales you it generates. If a tool is productive, keep using it.

What does it mean by "productive"? Being productive means giving you more than just a one-time deal. If it can draw new customers to return and do business with you again, then it makes economic sense to keep doing the same method. Remember, it costs a lot less to get returning customers to buy from you again than new ones do because they now have the confidence in and brand awareness with you. And if you can break even on advertising, that would be wonderful. For example, you spend $1,500 on marketing. At the end of your campaign, you've generated $4,000 worth of sales. Let's say all of your other costs (excluding marketing) are $2,400, your pre-marketing net profits would be $1,600. Now minus that profit with the cost of advertising ($1,600 - $1,500 = $100). You're now a little bit above breakeven. In this case, you could consider the marketing to be successful because now it will be a lot less expensive (or even free) to get those people to return in the future and buy from you again. And when they do, the profit margin will become pure profit without much marketing expenses.

Even if your marketing effort turns your profit into the negative zone, it may be okay as well, especially when your business brand new. Let's say you use $3,000 to advertise your free workshop/seminar for whatever expertise you have, in which you calculate the marketing cost to be $100

per attendant. During the event, people can buy your book at $30, or join a $10 membership program just to try out, but you're pressuring anyone to buy when they attend. In that case, you have the downside of not recuperating any of your marketing costs. But that's okay, as you should look at the costs as "investment"; your initial goal is to start a relationship with your audience. You offer them education of your topic in a broader way, and it builds up your credibility and authority in their eyes. You can then invite them to join events that focus on specific interests and other opportunities. If they already like what they learn in the free education session and eager to find out more, they may choose to attend further, and that's when you generate bigger revenue.

That brings us to the next concept – the lifetime value (LTV) of a customer. This is probably one of the most important number you need to figure out for your business, as it'll give you a benchmark in order to decide whether your marketing will pay for itself or not. A simple way to calculate lifetime value is as follow:

1) (Average amount clients spent with you) X (average number of times they purchase from you) X (average length of the business relationship) = gross revenue

2) Gross revenue minus "hard" costs of delivering your product or service (i.e. direct labour and product costs) but NOT your normal overhead (those that will be spent whether you have a customer or not) = gross profit

For example, if you run a tutoring business, working with small group classes:

- Gender Average charge per group or per month: $500

- Average number of groups joined per client: 2

- Average length of relationship: 24 months

- So, gross revenue were: $500 x 2 x 24 = $24,000

- "Hard" costs are 40%, so 60% left for gross profit (before office overhead): $24,000 x 0.60 = $14,400

This gross profit represents that every NEW client means on average $14,400 to your business over a 24-month period (i.e. LTV). Also keep in mind that, on average, every new customer refers 0.5 new customers, which will then increase your gross revenue by another $12,000 (= $24,000/2) and gross profit by $7,200 (= $14.400/2).

If you've been in business for a few years, you should be able to calculate the LTV of your customers, and you can always adjust your calculation accordingly when you have more updated data as your business progresses. But if you're new to your business, a good place to start is to gather your data from industry norms, and use that to calculate your LTV for yourself.

Knowing the LTV of a client allows you to make smart marketing decisions based on numbers, not emotion. You'll become more confident in giving away a bit to gain a lot more, such as offering guarantees, bonuses and incentives to attract new clients, or giving referral appreciation gifts for clients who send business to you. It will also show you how much you should invest in order to gain a new customer and to keep one that is about to leave. For example, if you already know the LTV of a customer is $14,400, and you're now present with two marketing options – one costs $600 per new customer, another $1,000 per new customer, which one should you choose to implement? Most people may choose to go with the cheaper $600 option and ditch the $1,000 one. However, I would suggest you do both. While the cheaper option seems to make business sense, the $1,000 is still a very good return on your investment. What if I tell you today, "If you give me $1000 today, and you'll get $14,400 over the next 2 years," would you think it's a good return? Of course! Because it's 1440% return on investment over 2 years, or 720% per year! That's why knowing the LTV of your customer and track your marketing cost is so important.

CHAPTER 6

CONNECT WITH YOUR AUDIENCE USING E-ZINES, FLYERS, AND RECEIPTS

The very first thing you must be able to do before your marketing efforts can yield any results is to connect with your audience. Connecting well with your audience first and your selling will become much easier. Otherwise, your sales efforts are doomed to fail because nobody will trust you or even know who you are. So what should you do to engage with them effectively? We have a few suggestions for you:

- Identify the characteristics of your ideal customers that you desire to acquire. You can refer to the list of factors that we've discussed in the previous chapter. Once you've written down as much information as you can discover, pin it up beside your desk. This will become the person you are writing to.

- Write it like a friendly conversation. Keep it fun and light with sense of humour. Keep it simple to read and understand by not using higher level English words or technical jargons. When you first start, you should keep writing let your chain of thoughts flow, and worry about editing later.

- Engage them with interactive experience, like questions and answers (Q&A), best photo contests, success stories sharing, featured customer of the month, etc.

E-ZINES

To start connecting with your customers with the above 3 steps, one of the best ways is to start a free online newsletter, also known as an e-zine. Why is it good to use? Because:

- Interactive; engaging with customers in different ways

- Good for communicating with a large group of people, yet in a personalized and intimate way

- Virtually FREE to do

- Easy to set up

- Little risk or pressure

- Show off your expertise

- Not "salesy"; you can simply focus on learning to connect with your audience

In fact, email communication is probably the best way for you to start practicing. We recommend sending one e-zine weekly or biweekly, and no more than that. Let's say you fix one day of each week or every other week (e.g. Friday) and send out your e-zine. That's a good setup because spacing out evenly and being consistent is crucial in building a relationship between you and your customers.

How do you start learning to write your newsletter? First, you need to study from the best people in the industry. In the field of sales and marketing, a copywriter is a professional who makes a living by writing advertising materials that inspire people to respond or take actions. They are the best people from whom you want to learn. By studying their work, you can learn their writing style, tone, feel, and approach, then you can try to incorporate into your own communication style. So with a library or online search, look for sales letters from copywriters that resonate with you, pick a time in a day where you can truly sit down and read their work, and learn those elements. Better yet, write them out by hand. This step may seem tedious, but writing it out can actually let you absorb their style, tone, and feel into your mind and body – it's like learning it by experiencing it. Once you get a feel of it, you can then do the exercise of adapting it to your own business needs. We're not suggesting that you go copy others' sales letters word for word; we're saying that, using the style and tone that you like and just learned, you create a piece that fits your own personality and business needs. You'll probably find it a lot more difficult than you think, but this practice will really get you think on the right track.

Before you produce your own marketing materials, there are 3 types of leads generation ads you need to practice writing, and you start from the short and easy one first:

1) Super short – 50 words or less; use this when you're writing pay-per-click ads, online classifieds, online directory listings, and newspaper classified.

2) Medium length – 100-500 words; you create it for magazine ads, print "placement" ads, or online reviews, etc.

3) Long – 1-2 pages; some examples would be full-page print ads, advertorials, or even 1-2 page online flyers. You use this type of lead generation to try to get your prospects to sign up for your e-zine in exchange for getting something for free, like e-book, audio, or video, etc.

When you write, make sure your ad connects with your audience first by presenting them with something that they want, and promoting at least one benefit of your offer. Your strategy is to offer them something for free in exchange for them to contact you and to lure them in.

For example, you can say, "You'll get an insightful report in [your subject] ABSOLUTELY FREE when you contact me now!" This will help you connect with your audience and inspire them to take action. From the responses you get, you'll know if you've done a good job or not. Once you're comfortable with writing smaller version of ads, you can do the same thing on a longer piece like a one-page flyer.

FLYERS

One-page flyer is one of the most under-utilized marketing type of newsletter because it usually takes more effort in creating one. But before you make one, you have to answer four important questions:

1) **Who are you addressing?** In another words, who are your targeted customers? What do they like and dislike? More importantly, what problems are they facing and how can your product or service help them? For example, business professionals aged 30-50 (white-collar workers) who need advice on business suits. This is the part where you have to do your due diligence in your research.

2) **Who are you trying to avoid?** Why would you need to avoid certain people? Because they are the ones who would waste your time, won't buy from you, or just don't want to have anything to do with you. And by choosing the right tone and words, you can attract certain people and repel certain others. For instance, anyone working in trades (blue-collar workers) who don't really need business suits for work.

3) **What do you want them to do?** Once they've read your flyer, what action do you want them to take? You don't want to offer too many choices of action because people would be confused. Limit to just one action to keep it simple. For example, you can ask them to "Come into the store to get a FREE consultation/recommendation on business wardrobes" based on their physiques.

4) **What will you give them in return for their action?** In our previous example, we're offering a free advice. Now with your own business, what would you give them? You're offering your ideal potential customers something useful or meaningful in order to motivate them to take action. You can think about product discount, free samples, free consultation, free report, draw, etc.

Once you're ready to start writing your actual sales piece, you can use the following steps to develop it with a logically approach:

1) Think of 3 (or more) benefits your customers will receive if they ever take the action you suggest. What rewards are they going to get if they follow your call? Now prioritize those benefits by putting yourself into their shoes, thinking objectively, and seeing which benefits seem to be the most appealing to them and which one is not. You'll then base your headline on your most appealing benefit (i.e. your #1 benefit), and this will set the overall tone and theme for the entire flyer. So let's say if you operate a fitness center, your top 3 benefits could be:

- Get a free 7-day trial membership

- Get free 1-hour fitness consultation

- Get a bundle discount if multiple people sign up under one membership plan

Your headline could look something like this: "Come In Today To Get Unlimited Gym Access For 7 days – Absolutely Free!"

2) Next, in the same order as you rate them, write a paragraph or two explaining why each benefit is great, and how it'll help solve their problems or make their lives better. For your opening sentence, re-state the information from your headline in a friendly, conversational tone, and then provide more details. Remember, to better connect with your audience, the focus of your writing is always on them – their experience, their feelings, and how you can help them. Put yourself into their shoes, and imagine their excitement when they feel better with your offer. Exaggerate that feeling and put them in words! The point is to keep the positive energy flowing when you're writing, so don't worry about editing until much later.

3) If you happen to have testimonials from your past clients, you would want to use them to showcase how good and trustworthy you and your business are. Pick out the best one(s), and use your judgment to make sure it looks good and easy to read.

4) In wrapping up your letter, you make your closing offer. How you close depends on your answers to question #3 (what you want them to take) and #4 (what they will get in return). Another important point here is to ALWAYS include a deadline! You want to create the urgency for them to take action immediately. The more time you give them, the more they'll think about it and procrastinate, and the more likely their memory and interest of it will be gone as time goes

by. So here is an example, "Come in to our gym before August 30, show us this flyer, and you'll get a complimentary 7-days trial membership. Plus, you'll get 1-hour free exercise consultation and a bundle discount if you and your friends sign up for membership at the same time." Then put your phone/fax number, address, website/email address so they can reach you.

5) The last piece of advice is, do not ask your family members or friends to read and evaluate your sales letters because they may not be part of your targeted audience who are interested in what you have to offer. You want to check with someone who actually has some marketing knowledge and experience, like a copywriter or marketer, so that you can get professional opinions even though they have no interest in it.

RECEIPTS

It's also important to nurture and even improve your customer relationships AFTER a sale. After all, you do want your customers to come back and buy from you again and again, don't you? One way to do this is

by using a receipt. How to do it? Well, it can be as simple as writing a few words on it! It can help you connect with your customers with almost no additional cost on your part because it's something you give to your customers on a regular basis anyway. If your receipt has nothing special other than the standard description of items and price amounts, then you're missing out on a big opportunity to connect with your folks.

A well-placed paragraph on your receipts you send to your customers can

- Create a personal connection which makes them feel special

- Prevent "buyer's remorse" by re-affirming that they've made the right decision

- Reduce your refund rate

- Pre-condition them to buy more and/or more often from you

And there are a few things you need to keep in mind before you start writing:

- Always focus on them, not you

- Keep it short and sweet

- Be sincere

- Keep a positive and appreciative tone

- Close by expressing your desire to serve them again in the future

Remember, when you're trying to connect with and foster your customer relationships, there are 3 main emotions that you need to touch:

1) **Trust** – Before any business transaction can take place, trust between the parties involved has to exist. No trust, no deal. No one likes to get scammed or ripped off. If you don't reassure your customers each step of the way, chances are they'll start assume the

worst. That's why it's very important to reassure them that they have made the right choice by choosing you for all their needs.

2) **Support** – If your clients know that you're doing your best to take care of them, they will feel nurtured and supported, which will make them relax and happy. A very important part of service business is to take responsibility of handling other people's affairs.

3) **Exclusivity** – Everybody wants to get full attention and be treated uniquely according to what and how they like; that makes them feel special. One way to create this special feeling with your clients is to let them know that you don't work with anybody; you only work with those whom you think are great fit and special to you (well, you should be doing that anyway). Once they know this, not only would they feel special, they will also feel lucky and privileged to have you serve them

If you ever get a mind block in coming up with words or phrases to connect those emotions and you feel frustrated, don't worry! Let's try the following exercise. On a piece of paper, draw a vertical line in the middle so you separate the paper with two vertical columns. At the top of the left column, you put down the word for one of the emotions – let's say "trust." Underneath it, write down any words that you think will associate with that emotion of trust. Now on the right column, with each word you've written down (on the left), try to come up with at least one thing your business does to make your clients

feel that emotion. For example, "total satisfaction or 100% money back guaranteed." You'll do the same exercise for the other two emotions.

Once you finish the whole exercise, you're now ready to write the "Customer Appreciation and Thank You" message for your receipt. Here is an example:

"Thank you for choosing John & Tim Tailor Company for your professional business wardrobe needs. We really appreciate your support. It's been an absolute pleasure serving you! This is a receipt for your records of services you have already paid for.

Here at John & Tim, we take pride in providing great service to a selected few who like choose the best to look the best! Call us old-fashioned, but we still think that giving you the time and attention you deserve can help us truly give you the look you want. We're lucky to have quality customers like you, and look forward to working with you again in the future!"

Now, your receipt isn't an accounting statement that simply reminds your customers of how much they've spent with you. With your short message, it will make them feel smart, appreciated, and supported, which will make them more likely to return for their future needs. To harness that power of connection, all it takes is some extra efforts on the receipt that you're going to send away anyway.

MEASURING YOUR RESULTS

Whether you use e-zines, flyers, or receipts, assessing the effectiveness of your marketing effort is ALWAYS important, so that you can see what works and doesn't work, and adjust your budget accordingly. If you're not sure how, here we have two suggestions for you:

1) **Return on investment (ROI)** – This measurement is based on the difference between the amount you invest in your marketing effort and the sales revenue you get. Let's say you operate the fitness center (from the previous example). You send out 500 sales flyers and each one costs you a total of $3.00 (includes printing, envelops and postage); you've invested a total of $1,500 in marketing flyers. If you have 50 new gym membership signups at $40 each, you'll have sales revenue of $2,000. Your ROI would be $2,000 minus $1,500, then divided by your initial investment, and you'll get a ROI of 33.3%.

2) **Response rate percentage** – This is the percentage of how many people respond versus how many people see your ad. Let's say you write (or send) 500 sales flyers and you get 50 new members sign up. Your response rate percentage would be 50/500, which is 10%. Realistically, is 10% a good response rate? It depends on the industry. But generally speaking, 10% on a cold list (people who have never heard of you before) is excellent!

So, with the tools we discuss in this chapter, not only can you connect with your audience, you can also inspire them to take action. Of course, getting them to take action you suggest is more important because, after all, the main goal for your business is to make money for yourself.

CHAPTER 7

GROW YOUR BUSINESS BY

ORGANIZING EVENTS

Other than advertising through electronic media and traditional mailing, one of the most effective ways to grow your business is to hold physical events for current and prospective customers. There are 3 types of events you can do:

1) Promotional events/demonstrations

2) Client appreciation events

3) Seminars/workshops/presentations

PROMOTIONAL EVENTS / DEMONSTRATIONS

Promotional events are the ones we see very often. It's usually used to tie with a big sale of the featured product or service. Instead of having the same old "sale" trying to sell your product, you turn it into an "experience." Recently, we've seen a very innovative promotional event for rescue pet adoption. It may not be a "sale" of product per se, but the idea of promotion is the same. There is an animal welfare non-profit organization in New York that holds an annual pet "catwalk" in a brewery. During this event, rescue animals will walk the catwalk in order to showcase them and promote their adoption. Silent auction will also take place to raise funds for the animal rescue groups that participate in the events. In the meantime, community members, fire and police departments can enjoy beers and socialize with each other (and those adoptable animals). This gives people a reason to come in besides just seeing a bunch of rescue animals.

This achieves multiple goals. First of all, you want to attract a lot of potential adopters who are really interested in getting pets. Second, you want to create "buzz" just to get a bunch of people to come out in general, in which some may turn into adopters. Third, you want to create a "warm fuzzy" feeling in people with opportunity for social interaction. So after they come to your event, when they are ready to get a pet, you will be the one who pops into their minds first. It would work even better if you can take down their contact information and keep in touch with them on a regular basis. Fourth, you want to create a "family" gathering. When both mom and dad come out, you'll have both decision makers there. This makes adoption much easier.

Now you may ask, "But I don't run an animal rescue organization, how can this strategy apply?" Trust me, it'll still work! Any business can hold events –think of a topic or product for your event and incorporate something fun into it – you'll have product promotion/sale, entertainment, food, and something to capture contact information of new people for future contact (e.g. draw).

CLIENT APPRECIATION EVENTS

Even if you have a business that doesn't normally have "sales," such as professional practice – you most likely won't see a physician seeing two patients for a medical fee of one, right? The "event" strategy can still work very well. In this case, you will hold a "Client/Patient Appreciation" event, and do the same thing as sales promotional events. Create a good reason for people to come in to your office and have some fun, like anniversary of your business, seasonal holiday, etc. But you won't be promoting your service hard to "cold" prospects; that would be seen as pushy and it'll be a turn-off. Instead, you should promote it to your past and current customers, and encourage them to bring their family and friends along. Wine and cheese gatherings and BBQ are great options.

In fact, you can work together with other non-competing businesses with similar target interests (e.g. doctor's office and medical supply company). You invite your clients and they invite theirs. Talking about synergy! Look at our animal rescue organization example again. They team up with a local brewery to hold an animal runway show. All parties (i.e. event organizer, rescue group, brewery, community, fire/police departments) invite their clients and friends to this fun and meaningful event. That in itself creates demand for the next one; people want to be invited to be part of the group doing something fun and worthwhile, and they look forward to participating again. If each party brings in just 10 people, there will be a total of 60 people – much easier than getting 60 people all by one single party. This doesn't even have to involve a "pitch" for any product or service (i.e. adoption or crafted beer). All you do is to "feature" them.

SEMINARS / WORKSHOPS / PRESENTATIONS

This last type of event that we'll be discussing is also probably the one that many people are afraid of because it involves public speaking in front of a group of audience. When all eyes are on you, you can't help but feel nervous and worry that you may make a fool out of yourself. While this is natural and understandable, public speaking is one of the most effective ways to grow your business because:

1) **Respect and credibility** – Everyone knows that public speaking isn't easy; some even compare that fear with the fear of death! It takes a lot of courage, confidence, and preparation to stand in front of a crowd and present your ideas in a coherent and enjoyable manner. This is why people who can do well in public speaking will

often get instant respect from their audience. Plus, a lot of inferred expertise is often placed on the speaker. Audience will automatically assume that the speaker must be an expert in the field so he/she is invited to speak on that topic.

2) **Leverage** – The respect, credibility, and the inferred expertise you gain from a large group of audience is something you cannot gain from a one-on-one coaching session. This will give you a big leverage in establishing your own brand and sell your product or services. People will now seek to hear from you or want to work with you. You should take advantage of that.

3) **Time-saving** – Time is money. Going over the same promotional speech to one single person at a time for several hundred times really seems like a waste of time. But with presentations, you can just do it once to several hundred people instead, so you can have more free time to do whatever is more important to you. Isn't that a lot more time efficient?

Now, for some of you, here comes the difficult challenge: the fear of public speaking! Well, if you just want to be able to do it and are willing to go out of your comfort zone, it's really not that difficult. All you need is to keep practicing in front of a mirror and a few friends (also get feedbacks). Over time, your confidence will develop, and it'll get easier and easier. But if you are completely new to public speaking and

you want to become professional in it, you should get started with quality training. One of the most well-known organizations is Toast Masters. You learn public speaking in a supportive environment where everyone is at the same level of skills and confidence as you, so it shouldn't be too scary.

If you are prefer to start doing public speaking with some company instead of doing it alone, you can organize events with some other non-competing business with similar target customers. That way you wouldn't be as nervous, and you can actually share your customers and attract their friends too.

As your credibility grows, you'll become the recognized expert in your field locally, and most importantly, you will make more money. Regardless of what business you're in, you can always find opportunities to do "show and tell" events to grow your business.

CHAPTER 8

CROSS-MARKETING WITH JOINT VENTURE

The business world has changed dramatically. In the past, businesses minded their own things and competed with each other to become bigger and better. But now businesses are not conducted in the same way anymore. The usual strategies like customer loyalty, low-cost advertising, and hard-selling simply aren't cutting it. These days, we've seen a lot more collaborations among big businesses; different industries with similar targeted group of customers often form strategic alliance (a.k.a. joint venture) to enjoy synergic benefits.

However, not many small- and medium-sized business owners use this strategy to combine forces together. Many of those owners are territorial, egocentric, and afraid of competition, which make them less willing to collaborate with others. We're in business to make maximum profit with the least amount of costs, time, and risks. But with their small mindsets, they end up working and risking too much for way too little. To change this situation, they first need to change their mentality, which is the most important. Prior to any strategic partnership with anyone, they need to understand the value of relationship, trust, and leverage. Not until their mentality changes are they suitable for joint venture, which is a practical and effective business system. Why? Because relationships, integrity, authenticity, and reciprocity are the factors that will determine the success of a joint venture.

Joint ventures allow any business owners in any industry or geographic location to maximize their profits and minimize their expenses in terms of costs, time, and risks. To ensure successful joint ventures, you'll need to keep 3 things in mind:

1) **Only partner up with the right people** – A right relationship to start is very important. Don't partner with people who are greedy or desperate for money because they will make and justify poor decisions. When you associate with them, your own reputation is on the line as well. Like it or not, you will be judged by who you keep. You also don't want anyone who has most of the control in resources (e.g. revenue, decision-making) in the joint venture; not only will you not get a say in how things should run, you may also get underpaid, or worse, not getting paid at all. Always work with someone who has the same work ethics as you, so you won't have to bear all the workload.

2) **Get the right training and support** – That's the reason why you read this chapter to learn how to do it properly. Also, go out and

meet someone who has past experience in joint venture and is willing to be your mentor, so you can learn from their secrets and mistakes.

3) **There must be a win-win reciprocity within the partnership** – Everyone has to win, meaning that with equal shares of inputs, everyone has to gain outputs he/she wants from it. That way, your hard work and payments will be rewarded based on foreseeable or pre-determined results, not speculative or empty promises. You won't get ripped off by so-called "consultants" and "coaches."

JOINT VENTURE STRATEGY

Want to make sure your next joint venture will be successful? We have a 5-steps blueprint for you:

Step 1: Find Out Other People's "Hot Buttons"

What is a "hot button"? It is a burning desire that everyone has, whether it's something they crave so badly, or a problem they needs to solve urgently. It doesn't matter if the person is rich or poor; everyone has something he/she wants, something that they are willing to pay for and they cannot justify their decisions logically.

To find that hot button, the most important thing you should do is to ask open-ended questions, listen closely, look for clues, and try to understand them at a deeper level. For example, what are their secret desires? What keeps them awake all night long? What do they love or fear? What's stopping them from getting what they truly want (e.g. financial hardship, guilt, embarrassment, priorities)? You need to know what it is in order for the partnership to work.

Step 2: Understand What You're Offering

Besides focusing on others' need, you need to know about yourself and your business as well. What product or service are you selling that has a high profit margin or life time value? Who do you want to sell to?

Or are you offering to someone who has influence, and you hope he/she can help your sale (i.e. influence marketing) and achieve mutual gains? How much commission are you prepared to pay then? How frequent will you pay it out (e.g. per transaction, ongoing basis, one-time only, or initial sale, etc.)? Is there anything you want to offer to your potential partner that is non-monetary as compensation instead? For example, buy them things they won't buy themselves, or reciprocate in other ways.

Lastly, you need to predict your closing ratio. In other words, if someone refers 10 qualified people to you, how many sales would you make, on average, conservatively? This is an important question, as it'll determine how much and how often you pay out your commission.

Step 3: Approach Your Potential Partner(s) To Test The Water

Once you know what they want, approach them for their interests or ask them to refer you to prospects you want to sell to. In return, you're offering them what they want (i.e. their Hot Button) for their effort and commitment.

Step 4: Get Into Details And Seal The Deal

When they've expressed interest in your idea of partnership, you'll then need to set up the system and disclose all necessary objectives, specifics, and details, so they know exactly what they have to do in order to get what they want. At the end, remember to ask them to repeat back what you've told them to ensure their understanding. Preferably, you would want to write down all the terms and conditions in black and white too.

Step 5: Monitor And Manage The System

When your system is up and running, you can't simply sit back, relax, and expect things will always turn out the way you want by itself. You have to measure its outcomes on a regular basis in order to properly manage the system and build/improve your relationship with your partner. You may want to consider the following for your system management: mode and frequency of communication, to-do checklist, milestones for completion and rewards, etc.

Joint venture demonstrates one mindset: you're not in business by yourself because you can leverage other people's resources to achieve a win-win scenario. With this system, you can remove some of your risk, boost your profits, add values to your clients, and outwit your competitors who go solo in their business venture.

CHAPTER 9

NETWORKING IS THE KEY TO YOUR MARKETING SUCCESS

Relationships are the key to riches. Why? When you look at successful people, you'll see that they all have successful relationships with various people around them, such as mentors, business partners, suppliers, employees, and customers. Nobody can win on his/her own; their surrounding people are the ones who contribute to his/her success. Thus, creating a successful network is strategically important because it helps cultivate your social connections and allows you to monetize your return of investment.

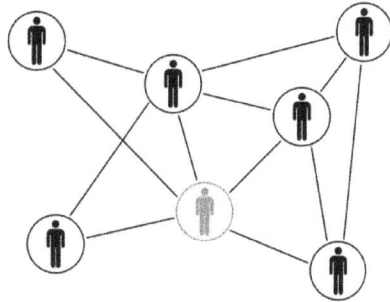

As we've already discussed, the cost of getting a new client is huge. For example, advertising in newspapers and magazines to a broad audience will produce an average of 1-3% response ratio, which is very inefficient. And that's just a response, not actual sales. This option is expensive and simply unaffordable for a start-up or small business. That's why we've been advocating direct response marketing all along. The best return on your investment is obtained from your existing customers; not only they've done business with you before and the trust factor is already there, they will also bring in new customers through word-of-mouth, which is by far the most powerful form of advertising since third party referrals have enormous credibility.

While we all know why networking is important, knowing how to do it properly may be another story. So, in this chapter, we'll give you an overview of how you can tap into your network and start getting results.

MEETING FOR THE FIRST TIME

When you meet someone for the very first time, very often you'll be polite, and have a causal chat or exchange basic information about each other. But that's just the beginning of building a new connection. Other than being sincere and genuine, you'll also need to help and empower others in order to get the most out of any relationships.

So from now on, when you meet someone new and exchange business cards, listen and write down 3 things about them that have nothing to do with what's on their business cards. For example, what sports do they play? What hobbies do they have? Where are they planning for their trip? How many kids do they have? Write down anything except their jobs. At the end of the day, their careers don't define who they are, and everyone's life is unique. You need more personal information beyond the surface to build a deeper connection and to influence their social behaviours and mindsets. That's what makes a connection more powerful than simply collecting business cards and asking the standard question about what they do for living.

FOLLOW UP

Next, you then need to follow up within 24 hours. Listen to what they say, and mention 1, 2, or all 3 of those non-job items during your conversation. The idea here is to show that you pay attention to what they had said, and try to add value to their lives. Do you have the ability to solve a problem for them? If not, can you direct them to an appropriate resource? For example, if they are looking to book a trip to Cuba, do you have any good recommendation in where to stay and what to do? Don't underestimate the power of following up; this simple act can set you apart from the crowd of mediocrity. Most people don't continue with their effort to connect, the momentum from the initial meeting will just die off, and the connection is lost.

The main purpose in building relationships and network is to create for yourself more leverage, which is defined as other people's money, time, and resources. The more people you have in your network, the more potential leverage you can use for future. However, that doesn't mean you go crazy in collecting business cards from everybody you meet. Remember, collecting business cards and being superficial won't even get you solid relationships. What you should do is to stay focus and really engage with your core 200 people and let the third degree of separation works for you.

CONVINCER AND MOTIVATION STRATEGIES

Before a value exchange of money, time, and resources can take place, sufficient intangible value has to be exchanged first. So next, you need to invite and engage these new relationships into your life by repeatedly using the Convincer and Motivation Strategies.

In Neuro-Linguistic Programming (NLP), Convincer Strategy is a tactic based on how a person comes to believe something to be true, since everyone has different reaction to one particular event or thing. For some people, they may need to see or read it with their own eyes in order to believe it. For others, they need to hear something a few times from a few people first before they believe it. Basically, it's about how the mode and frequency of reception before you believe certain thing is true.

So when it comes to influencing people, the Convincer Strategy becomes one of the most important and useful strategies because knowing how to make them trust can pave way to success for you. You might not have all the stories, data, facts and figures on hand, but if your targeted audience is hearing it in the way they expect it (i.e. matching their Convincer Strategy), then you will be saving your breath. For instance, in one project that we worked on, one of the managers wasn't open to our suggestions that could enhance the efficiency of the business operation. We went in to the meeting, prepared with relevant research findings and good answers for their questions. However, after a few meetings with the same data and answers, that manager accepted and incorporated our suggestions into his planning. From hindsight, you can see that time for consideration was the determining factor in the decision making. By allowing enough time, you matched that person's Convincer Strategy.

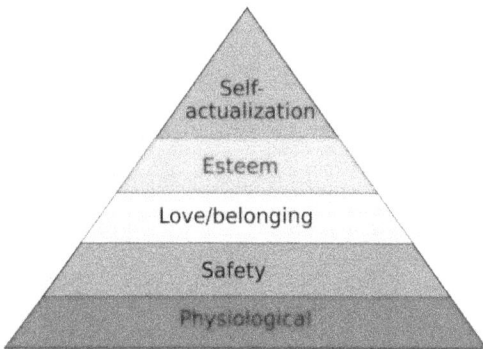

After you've gained their trust and they have opened up to you, you'll then need to motivate them to keep connecting with or knowing more about you. Their motivation may come from various sources – psychological needs, security, sense of belonging, self-esteem, or self-actualization. When you google Motivation Strategies, you'll see that there are numerous of them. Which one to use depends upon the characteristics or needs of your audience. For example, if you're an auto mechanic and your clients/followers have problems with their automobiles, you can give out some of your expertise (in form of advice/tips/review) for free in your conversation or regular newsletters.

Now, after all your effort in gaining trust and getting a sale or referral, you need to capture those opportunities instead of continuing in acquiring news one. By this time, your clients are probably praising about you or your business, and sharing you with everyone they know. This means it is time to cultivate such a good reputation. And remember, good news travels fast, but bad news travels faster. So make sure you don't anything for short-term gain at the expense of long-term relationships.

Your core values in business are all about your personal core values. Take time to communicate your core values to your client, and get them to buy into it because time and repetition are crucial in building strong relationships. You may then have a question, "how can you build strong relationships with many people when you only have so little time in meeting?" This is when you need to your "stuntman" in networking – a newsletter.

A newsletter written in a casual format and sent out on a regular basis is all that is required to attract, build, and maintain your client basis. As you get more and more people in your network, money and opportunities will come to you. Over time, your audience will unconsciously perceive you as reliable and credible, and this will make you worthy of notice and outstanding from the crowd. Doing business comes down to trust, and people trust predictability and consistency. As for how to write newsletter, you should refer to our next discussion in the book.

It's true that you get back what you put out. If you deliver value upfront, you'll attract value people. You're not and should not be in business for sales transactions; you should be in business for lifetime of value transactions. The lifetime value of just one person is priceless. That's why you need to get connected and stay connected.

CHAPTER 10

HOW TO USE NEWSLETTERS

FOR YOUR MARKETING

In the previous chapter, we talked about using newsletter as your "stuntman" for your marketing. Not only would it create a sense of belonging in your clients, it would also keep you in front of your clients and prospects without hassling or pitching them, or using the traditional advertising that goes into one ear and out from another. More importantly, it is the cheapest and most effective way to deliver your message to your clients.

We all know that, as every business owner, we know that we need to keep engaging with our customers. Otherwise, they will forget about us over time and stop doing business with us. Mind you, even if you do everything right, you'll still lose customers every year due to no fault on your own. It can happen for various reasons, such as moving away, death, or no longer need of your goods and services. Now you see why it's so important for us to keep in touch.

We know you may have questions or doubts about using or even making newsletters. So let us address them for you. For example:

- **Newsletters don't apply to my business** – That's not true at all. We've seen newsletters being used for all kinds of businesses, like chiropractors, financial planners, auto mechanics, B2B, B2C, or retail industry, and the list can go on. You could and should use a newsletter not just to keep your business alive, but to grow it as well. At the end of the day, business is all about people talking to people. Whether we're business owners or customers, we all prefer the "human touch" as a way of connection, accountability, and reassurance.

- **I don't know what to write for each month** – It's daunting to write anything if you don't even know what to write in the first place, not to mention doing it in a monthly basis. But with the help in this chapter, you'll have no problem. So keep reading.

- **I'm not good at (or don't like) writing at all** – You're not trying to become an author for a novel here. Don't compare yourself with famous authors for books like Harry Potter or Lord of The Ring. The trick here is to write exactly as how you speak; if you wouldn't say it, don't write it. And don't try to pretend to be someone you're not either. If you're not a funny person, don't try to crack jokes in print.

- **I don't have time to write** – Let's be honest, who will ever have enough time for everything every day? Nobody does. We've all got family, friends, work, daily chores, etc. But if there is a will, there is a way. If you want it to happen so badly, you'll find a way to make it happen.

- **I'm just starting out and I have no mailing list** – That's understandable, especially when you first start your business. Getting the full name, address AND permission of every prospect you meet is very important, and we'll show you how to do that.

- **I'm broke and I don't have a lot of money** – Yes, there will be some setup costs to doing a newsletter (e.g. printing, envelopes, and stamps), but compare with other forms of physical advertising, it actually require relatively little money. You can do it on demand with your home printer, and if you have only $15 to spend on marketing today, you can still send our 25 newsletters, which is better than not doing it at all.

- **I already send out regular electronic newsletters (e-zines) to my clients** – That's great, but keep in mind that spam filters are picking out almost half of those emails. Even with those that pass through the filter, they may not get read, or printed out and passed around, because e-zines have no intrinsic value. Emails are efficient in reaching more people in short amount of time, but they are not

nearly as effective in motivating people to take action – that's the big difference. So if you're gaining traction and brand awareness through emails, that's a good start. But if those intangible reactions don't lead to actual transactions in forms of cash in the pocket, they're still futile and you'll need something more. After all, online comments and feedbacks cannot pay the bills on your hand.

While you see problems with creating or using newsletters, it's important for you to recognize the reasons why newsletters can be such a powerful tool that works like a charm. For instance:

- **It keeps you in the minds of your customers** – Just because we can sell to our prospects doesn't necessarily mean they will do business with us. Remember the time when you see something cool online that you want to buy, but then your phone rings, or you need to measure what size you need, or you're in a hurry to leave the house – basically life gets in your way – then you procrastinate in buying it at that moment or forget about it until much later. The bottom line is, with newsletter on a regular basis, your name and product/service will always be fresh in your clients' minds. Even though they don't or can't do business with you now, when they do need the product/service of your type, your name will pop up right away, as opposed to scratching their heads and feeling unsure which provider is good.

- **It'll give you maximum positioning** – Newsletters allow you to project the image you WANT the clients to have of you and your business. Although you shouldn't pretend to be something you're not (e.g. an international conglomerate with a 20,000+ staff when you're just a start-up with 2 people), you can still use newsletter to polish up your image to become a field professional or industry expert.

- **It allows a non-salesy communication** – Newsletter allows us to keep in touch with your customers and prospects without being salesy and making them feel like they're being pitched all the time. You can treat your communication with them with a degree of respect for their time and still run a profitable business. Include a "how to DIY" or "joke of the day" section, making it a more interesting way to drive your business.

- **It's a great bonding tool between you and your customers** – When you do it right, newsletters will become a bond between you and your clients, and over time, they will miss it when you miss sending out one issue.

- **It can be passed along** – Newsletters can be passed from person to person, especially when you make it so funny, interesting, or worthwhile that people want to share the laugh or information with others. This means that even if your contact person leaves, you still have a presence with people in their social circle.

- **Newsletter materials can be recycled** – Bet you don't know that newsletter materials can be recycled, do you? You can actually use previous newsletter articles for blog posts, and vice versa. All you have to do is to re-word them. That will ease some concerns that you may have a hard time coming up new things to write on a regular basis.

- **It's scalable** – You can start off small and simple by using your home printer and buying some envelopes and stamps. As your business grows to a certain level, you can outsource this to a third party so they can print the newsletters out and mail them for you.

Remember that one of your doubts about making newsletters is the lack of a mailing list? How can you possibly build a list – and build it fast – when you just start your business? Here is an idea: get a booth at a local business expo, and have a draw with awesome prize.

Use a big sign (bigger than your company name) and make it attractive so you can get people's attention from far away. As for the prize, you can't be cheap here; make sure you have something that makes this draw irresistible, so put in some serious thoughts. However, you'll want something that you don't sell in your booth because some people may put off buying your product if they know they might win it instead.

Also, you and your staff need to push the effort on everyone who come by and playfully drag them over to enter the draw. More importantly, never leave the forms out for them to fill out themselves; chances are they won't have initiative to even pick up the pen. You've got to be proactive about this! On the entry form, be sure to get full contact information, including phone, mailing address, email, etc. Not only should you put a bold line that says "FILL THIS IN PROPERLY! INCOMPLETE FORMS ARE INVALID!!" you also need to tell them to fill it out completely. Don't be surprised that, with such effort, a full 1/3 of the entries won't be as complete as you would want them to be.

Obviously, not everyone you meet will be qualified as your prospects. Some may not have the intention to work with you, while you may not want to work with some others for whatever reasons. So you'll need a method to sort them out on the spot, and that will save you time from doing it with a bunch of entries at the end of collection. We suggest you to use a "2-color form system." After you chat with them for a while, you can get a feel of whether you'll be working with them or not. Use one color form for the qualified prospects, and a different color for unqualified prospects. Don't worry about the need for precise sorting here; you're not trying to target for the perfect prospects, you're trying to save your time later on by trimming out the obvious ones. For the purpose of the draw, even though you have the unqualified ones, you should still make them legit. Keep all the entry forms in the bin for the draw, and make them all eligible for winning as long as their forms are filled out completely. And you'll then announce the prize winners in your first issue of the newsletter.

After the expo, you'll instantly have a list of suitable prospects, with the unsuitable ones taken out. See? Coming up with a mailing list isn't as hard as you think. You just need a way to entice people to you give you their information.

Now your next big hurdle is the content – what you should put in your newsletters. The very first thing that you have to always keep in mind is the purposes of your newsletter, which are to:

- Keep in contact with your client base (without selling)

- Keep you in front of your clients' minds

- Position yourself as the industry expert

- Generate a call to action

- Provide ongoing client education

Those would be the core purposes. Whatever you write, the contents have to revolve around the core. So in each issue, you'll have a "lead story," in which you provide an update to current events. Then for the rest of the newsletter, you'll have "monthly columns." These columns should complement you as a person and your business to the greatest extent possible. For example, if physical fitness training is your business, you can write about diet tips, cooking receipts, or various workout techniques and supplements. However, within each newsletter, there are 3 vital points that you must include (all or any one of them):

1) Testimonials – this is the most important!!

2) Customer of the month profile, or customer story wherever possible

3) Monthly/seasonal special

Besides those crucial ones, there are certainly many more topics that can go into your newsletters to make them more interesting and appealing. Here are some examples:

- Staff of the month profile

- Reviews for books, movies, music

- Reviews for restaurants, travelling

- Tips of the month (business, household, family)

- Crossword puzzles or Sudoku

- Cooking recipes

- Horoscopes

- Jokes

- This month in history

- Calendar of events

- Trivia questions

- Education about your business or related services/industry

Notice that a majority of these columns can be done for the entire year in one shot. That will leave you with only the monthly lead article, which can be done in just a few of hours and can save you a lot of time later on.

Besides, it's much easier to sit down for one day and finish all 12 issues-worth of column materials at once than to start one issue from scratch every month for 12 months. Don't you think so? To help you even further, let us give you other useful tips/advices in making newsletters.

- **Use a template** – The word programs in Windows/Mac have many great templates that you can use, and there is a lot more available online. Select one that you like to work with, and you can copy and paste the content for each month.

- **Any paper size is fine** – A regular 8 ½" x 11" printer paper with double-sided printing would be a good start. If you have a lot to write or want to include many nice pictures, you can use a 11" x 17" paper. Regardless what size you use, don't wait until you figure out the "perfect" paper size for you; just get it done.

- **Color of paper doesn't really matter** – We've seen black and white, blue, and green paper. Color isn't all that important as long as it doesn't hurt people's eyes from reading it (e.g. red).

- **Coated paper is very important** – We always use laser paper; the coating allows us to use thinner papers, while still having a nice look and feel. That makes a big difference on the hands of your customers.

- **Don't worry about formatting** – Similar to paper size, you should worry too much about formatting like margins and fonts. Keep it simple, consistent, and easy to read and reproduce; use one font and size for headlines or titles, another font and size for the body, and occasional bolds and italics for emphasis. Nothing too flowery or decorative. Understand that changes to the format will be inevitable as the style of your newsletter keeps evolving over time.

- **Develop your character or personality** – This is about positioning yourself. You need to think about your own character development because you want to convey to your audience the type of person you are, and that you're real. You can include a little psychological "anchor" to help your clients remember you better. For example, we know a fitness trainer here who has created and consistently advertising his slogan – "What time is it? It's SHOWTIME!" – on all of his promotions. It gives me an impression that he's confident about his body and knowledge. So now when people remember his face, they will immediately think of his slogan, and vice versa.

- **Use a lot of picture** – These days pictures and videos will attract more attentions than words alone. Since you can't put videos on papers, use relevant pictures wherever you think they will fit. And speaking of pictures, avoid the "real estate agent" type of head shot, especially the one with head title, because it looks too static and boring. Pictures that look like you're doing something are intrinsically more interesting.

- **Don't sacrifice contents for logos, graphics, and photos** – Yes, you use lots of pictures to make your newsletters more visually appealing, but you should never use them in place of quality contents. Pictures attract people visually, while contents educate or inspire them in a psychological level. That's why pictures are always secondary to contents.

- **Be aspirational but not bragging** – You need to write in a way that makes them want to be like you or take part in whatever is going on with you. But be careful not to brag about your work or achievement too much. Remember, the existence or survival of your business is about serving your clients' needs. You should focus on them, not yourself.

- **Speak in an inclusive and welcoming tone** – Whenever possible, use the word "we" instead of "I." You want to make your readers feel they're part of your group (i.e. you guys are together). Besides, the word "I" sounds like you're an egomaniac, which doesn't give you a good impression.

- **Always write with contractions** – For example, "there's" not "there is," or "you're" not "you are," etc. It will sound more conversational to your readers.

- **Make your newsletters entertaining** – You need to make it so good that they would miss it if it doesn't show up next month, and so irresistible that they want to share it with their friends. The last thing you want is to make it dry, in which people would toss it into the garbage bins as soon as they receive it. You may be a boring person in real life, but your marketing has to be interesting and likeable for it to become effective.

- **Provide full contact information** – This is a very important part but people seem to forget about it at least once. If you miss it, how can your current or prospective clients come to you when they want to? If you include a map to your business, that would be even better.

- **Read your newsletters out loud during proof-reading** – When you read it in your head, you'll tend to overlook some mistakes because you already know what you've written, and your brain will subconsciously override what you see with that knowledge. It's weird but it's true. That's why you should read it out loud when you proof-read; you can pick up mistakes by hearing as if someone is reading it to you.

- **Home printing first, outsourcing later** – When you first start, use your own computer and laser printer to print newsletters. Once you get past 24-36 newsletters, you should start looking into the costs (e.g. laser toner, paper, etc.) and determine whether home printing or having someone print for you (e.g. Vistaprint, Staples, Office Depot) is more economical. If you ever get to printing 2000+ a month, you should definitely look into having your newsletters done on a proper printing press.

- **Envelope vs. self-mailer** – We prefer envelopes so we have more space to include other sales materials, price sheets, etc.

Remember previously we said that you may be a boring person but your marketing can't be boring? The truth is, once you're committed to writing newsletters, you'll soon figure that the two actually can't co-exist. When your life is as uninteresting as a pond of dead water, you may be okay to write for a month or two, but then you will use up your "materials" with nothing new to write about. That's when you realize you should better go and do something interesting so you can have more interesting topics for your newsletters. Next thing you know, your life will become more interesting too! So here is the takeaway lesson: not only it can grow your business, it can also grow your personal life too! That's why you should get started on it now.

ABOUT THE AUTHORS

PATRICK NG

Patrick is an "Octopus" professional with diverse educational background and career experience.

He was in 4 different university programs in university: Bachelor of Pharmacy, Bachelor of Commerce (Finance), Bachelor of Arts (Drama and Foreign Language), and MBA (International Business). He loves the diversity in his learning, even though they all seem to be unrelated to each other.

As Vice-President in Marketing for Project Management Institute Northern Alberta Chapter (PMINAC), he was responsible for upholding the chapter's brand image and sponsorship drive, and extending its reach within the profession of project management. Meanwhile, he worked as a marketing consultant and event speaker, helping people with branding, positioning, and promotional needs for their businesses or personal careers. He believes that branding is emotional; a successful marketing campaign must be able to psychologically "move" people to come to you, rather than hard-selling them your product or service. And this is where his marketing experience can help.

In addition, since he was originally born in the international financial city of Hong Kong, he has always been interested in finance and real estate investment, and hasn't stopped learning ever since. During his education in Bachelor of Commerce after-degree and subsequent MBA degree, he enriched his body of knowledge in investment by taking real estate investment courses, and participating in various workshops on how to invest and raise capital for real estate. He also loves to talk about investing in stocks and foreign currency exchange, and exchange ideas with others.

With a passion to help others succeed, he gave out educational presentations, and later teamed up with his fellow MBA alumnus, Larry Yakiwczuk, to develop this "Magic Mirror" book series so they can help educate more people with their wealth of knowledge and experience.

ABOUT THE AUTHORS

LARRY YAKIWCZUK

Larry Yakiwczuk is the founder and owner of the Buckaru Group of Companies. He has 6 University Degrees, 30 years of real-estate investing experience, 15 years' experience trading derivatives, and has been financially free for the past 15 years. His proprietary investing strategies allow his investors to achieve significant returns on a consistent basis, regardless of the current market conditions. His mission is to educate the small investor and help them achieve their own financial goals!

Larry started his real estate investing career in the early 1980's while he was still in his twenties and attending University. He has extensive experience in all aspects of real estate investing including various forms of residential rental real estate as well as various forms of commercial real estate, including warehousing and industrial complexes. Recently he's been concentrating more on investment placement and management for his real estate investors. He concentrates on projects that will give his investors significant and consistent returns regardless of the current market conditions.

His experience in the single-family residential area began as most people's experience begins, that's with small houses and condos. He started out by buying individual housing units. He also started with some small Condominiums as well. He concentrated on all aspects of managing those properties including finding new tenants, property management, and eventually reselling the properties when the market was higher than it was when he bought them. At one point he started to specialize in small rental Condominiums. He found a great deal on the MLS that was listed by a realtor that specialized in this area. After he bought the first unit from this realtor, they struck a bond together, and since then, whenever that Realtor had a unit that fulfilled Larry's criteria, the agent would call Larry directly rather than listing the unit for sale to the public. The realtor knew that after he gave Larry the pertinent information he would have a yes or no answer on that same phone call. This resulted in Larry obtaining 10 Condominiums within the same high rise condo complex, and resulted in Larry owning approximately 15% of the entire complex. He then sat as president on the condo board and was able to effectively control the whole complex.

Larry also was able to obtain bank foreclosures directly from the bank because of the good banking relationships that he had established. An example of this is a 15 unit condominium complex that he obtained from the bank as a result of a foreclosure. He was actually able to get the foreclosing bank to fund his purchase of the property. He managed that property for a number of years, and finally resold the units individually for a substantial profit. He also has experience with purchase, management, and sale of small apartment buildings as well. He started off with small 8 and 15 unit apartment buildings that were actually not in his local area but were located in small residential communities around the Edmonton area. This gave him extensive training in dealing with long-distance management of commercial residential properties.

Larry has extensive experience in the area of true commercial properties such as warehousing and Industrial complexes. With these types of properties, he was able to gain experience in commercial leasing and negotiation techniques. He has experience in this type of commercial properties, both as an investor and as an end user. He currently owns a number of commercial warehouse buildings that are being used for his auction company business as well as other businesses.

In one case, he purchased a warehouse property for use in his auction business; however, he quickly realized that the property would generate more cash flow by being rented out to a local trucking company. A couple of years later, he sold that property to a competing trucking company for a significant profit.

Larry is now more concerned about investment management, and purchasing properties and managing them for his investors. He specializes in two forms of investor participation in his projects. The type of investor participation in his real estate projects is determined by the needs of the investor.

If an investor is concerned mostly with cash flow from his investments, then a mortgage investment is the investment of choice. This type of investment will give Larry's investors consistent cash flow over extended periods of time regardless of what is happening in the markets and is not dependent on a property being sold any time in the future. This type of investment is particularly suited to investors that need to live of the cash flow from their investments, such as retirement funds. Whether it is retirement funds are straight cash, Larry always has mortgages available to place investor funds.

The second form of investment Larry participates with his investors is in the form of equity or a joint venture partnership. In this type of investment, the investor is actually part owner of the property. In this case, there is generally no cash flow to the investor during the time of the investment however the investor does participate in the equity appreciation of the property and sees significant returns when the property is eventually sold. This type of investment is more suited to the younger investor, or the investor that simply wants to park his capital for a period of time and is not dependant on the cash flow from the investment. The returns on this type of investment are generally higher than the mortgage investments, but take longer to realize.

Because of his vast experience in the real estate and investment industries, Larry is always willing to talk to anybody about investing in real estate. If you have available cash and are ready to make an investment, please contact him directly.

6 BONUSES

5 Homes to Financial Freedom   FREE
A webinar recording explaining how you can achieve financial freedom with the equivalent cash flow of 80 rentals from owning just 5 homes. (Value of $49.99)
Visit **www.MagicMirrorInvesting.com/book**

Making Real Money With Joint Ventures   FREE
A webinar recording discussing the specifics about joint ventures and how they can be a short cut to vast residual profits with very little initial work. (Value of $49.99)
Visit **www.MagicMirrorInvesting.com/book**

Rent To Own with No Money and No Risk   FREE
A webinar recording with over 60 minutes on rent to own secrets and different ways to increase your profits and minimize risks in real estate investing. (Value of $49.99)
Visit **www.MagicMirrorInvesting.com/book**

A Millionaire's Mindset   FREE
A webinar recording giving you an insight into the mindset of a millionaire where you will learn a bit about business, real estate, and the stock market. (Value of $49.99)
Visit **www.MagicMirrorInvesting.com/book**

Power Investing   FREE
A webinar recording giving you an insight into the mindset of a Millionaire where you will learn a bit about the stock market and investing. (Value of $9.99)
Visit **www.MagicMirrorInvesting.com/book**

Educational Grants and Credits: FREE
We have a special educational grant program which helps students with the purchase of Advanced Educational materials. Also, any purchase of our related advanced educational programs or products, will result in the same amount returned as a fee credit on a major internet auction site that you can use for various listing upgrades or on site advertising. (Value up to $3,499.99)
Visit **www.MagicMirrorInvesting.com/book**